A Prospect of Poetry and Prose

A Prospect of Poetry and Prose

CW01506601

Poetry and Prose

by the

Liden Writers' Group

AUTHORS:

Dona Allen, Irene Berridge, Andrea Cook, Alan Fryer, Ross Kitchen,
Rosemary Lewis, Lindy O'Leary, Graham Vaughan, and Jenny Weeks

with contributions from

Margaret Fryer

and

Ann Perrin

COVER ART:

Julia V. H. Fryer

Dedication

Dedicated to our families, to the Prospect Hospice in Wroughton, Wiltshire, and to all the staff of Prospect past, present and future.

Since 1980, the Prospect Hospice has provided dedicated end-of-life care to local people around the clock, every day of the year. All profits from this book will be donated to the Prospect Hospice.

Table of Contents

Introduction

The Liden Writers' Group is a small group of writing enthusiasts who meet every Friday in Liden, a suburb of Swindon.

We write poems and short stories. Sometimes we set ourselves a theme, such as "write a poem or story including these three words". Our founder Irene has a tin containing lots of little pieces of card, each with a word printed on it. Sometime she gives us our three words by passing the tin around the table and getting people to pull out cards.

Many of the writings in this book have been broadcast on Swindon 105.5.

There is one chapter for each author, but we start off with a couple of chapters devoted to particular themes that we have set ourselves from time to time.

About Us

It was only through being nosey that Liden Writers' Group was born when, during an afternoon visit to the Liden Library in 2013, instead of selecting a book to read I watched people putting up boards and boxes. I asked one of the gentlemen to tell me what was going on, and he explained that the library was asking for new ideas of how to use their facilities. So there and then I suggested a writers' group. I had completed several writing courses at New College, and though I had enjoyed them immensely I no longer enjoyed being a 'night owl' once a week. To my surprise my idea was taken on board. I had to come up with a plan quickly and once that was done we were formed. Rosemary was waiting patiently to join. Sadly that first meeting comprised just the two of us. However we persevered and our numbers grew. Understandably members come and go as individual commitments vary yet I am pleased to say that the group has survived the odds.

Liden Library was our home for many years. We loved the atmosphere of people walking around us and sometime I am sure they listened while we read our pieces. Sometimes we whispered our pieces, though really we had nothing to worry about. We loved the librarians forever helping us with any queries.

And then, as we all know, Covid reared its head, but we were determined to keep going. After trying various online sites, our weekly video sessions got underway. They were quite a lifeline for us. And, as restrictions eased and the weather stayed glorious, we met on the grass outside! And so Liden Writers' Group survived and has flourished.

To be a writer you need a pen and some paper (even backs of envelopes have often come in handy). And many thoughts, memories, imaginations. We have spun many a tale over the years, enjoyed much laughter formed many new friendships, and thousands of words have been written. So what better time than now to stretch ourselves further and write a book. One step further and we have dedicated it to a worthy and very much needed cause, the Prospect Hospice.

As a writing group, this is our first venture into producing a book. We hope that when you turn the pages you might see the care we have taken to give you many enjoyable hours of reading. Key players in its creation were Alan and Dona for the many hours they spent in juggling with words and pages and Ross for his invaluable publishing knowledge and guidance, and then all of us - Rosemary, Andrea, Dona, Graham, Irene, Jen, Lindy, Alan and Ross, for the brilliant stories and poems.

Lastly a large thank you to Julia who provided the artwork.

This work of art has taken several months to plan and nurture and it is hoped that you, the reader, will enjoy the outcome.

Irene Berridge January 2025
Liden Writers' Group

Challenge 1 - The Garage

One week we set ourselves the task of writing on the theme "the garage".
Here are some of our resulting pieces.

The Garage

My husband is a hoarder, of that I'm very sure
You see, we have a double garage and you can't get through the door
Once in you scuttle sideways, like a crab along a beach
And everything I really need is way up out of reach
It has even got a second floor, who knows what's stored up there
I've often suggested we throw things out, but then I get that stare
He will then explain in detail, why he keeps so much stuff
That some bits are sentimental, so to chuck them would be tough
He says when he retires, he will start to clear things out
But if this actually happens, I really am in doubt
There is over 35 years of marriage
Piled up inside that garage
Prams, bikes, tools and cables
Paint, wood, a scarifier and old garden tables
But the plus side is, if I need something quite quick
He will drop what he is doing and into the garage he will nip
Then out he comes with a great big smile
Holding aloft that much needed green tile
This he tells me is why he won't throw things away
Knowing that it might be needed at any time, any day

Andrea Cook – 2024

The Garage

The house is pretty decent
The garden not too bad
The garage was a double
Took everything we had

The floor began to crumble
Cement turned to dust
Flat became uneven
Repairing was a must

My neighbour's had the same
The builders got it wrong
Chasing the developers
To rush the job along

The floor was put to rights
It took them just a week
But now that it's all sorted
The roof has sprung a leak

Dona Allen - 2024

Garage

Away for the day
All on his own
No worries or cares
Sat in a garage
Nobody around
Tools at his side
Engines in racks
All labelled and clean
He puts on a cap
Pulls out a watch
A flick of a switch
Movement breaks out
A train trundles by
Much to his delight
Hidden in his den
A childhood dream come true

Ross Kitchen - 2024

Illustrated by R Kitchen

The Garage

Several decades ago I helped out at weekends at a garage on the main road to Torquay. It's all changed now with bypasses etc but this story brought back memories although the story itself is pure fiction.

I don't really have a name. Sometimes I get called 'It'. Sometimes I get called Moggie. But normally I'm called The Garage Cat which is a long name but I don't mind. Evidently there is this new moosical out called Cats. Jed the garage owner wanted to call me Messo something but Angela his wife said I didn't belong to them and anyway it was a daft name and too long. Jed said I didn't belong to anyone and I was always there. Angela said worse luck but I'm not sure what she meant. She doesn't like me. I don't care. As for a name I don't even know what a moosical is. Except it sounds like a cow. Jed called Angela a cow once. I didn't understand. She doesn't look anything like a cow with her permed hair and red lips. Anyway she didn't like it. She slapped Jeff's face and then he said sorry and called her Angie. She liked that. There's an Angie that appears on their picture box nearly every evening. That Angie has a husband called Den and he always shouts at his Angie. Jed has only ever shouted at his Angie once and he really regretted it.

Jed and Angie like moosicals. Angie has a long cardigan made of lots of different coloured wool. Jeff calls it her multicoloured dream coat after another moosical they went to. Angie loves that cardigan but not as much as I do. If she leaves it on the chair in the garage shop by the till I jump up and curl myself into it. It's so warm and snuggly although I do get my claws caught up in it sometimes. That's when she stops calling me 'It' and calls me something else in a shouty voice. I understand the "You little" but the word that follows isn't very nice and anyway I'm a very clean cat. I never use the garage forecourt. I always use the field at the back. Actually the field at the back is where the mice come from. They smell the human food in the little garage shop. Even Angie has to admit I'm a very good mouse catcher. When Angie found the nibbled Shredded Wheat box and a trail of crumbs in the shop Jeff told her they were definitely keeping the stray. That was me. They argued a bit but I'm still here. I would have stayed anyway. I had nowhere else to go except for the cardboard box they found me in and I didn't want to go back in there.

I like belonging to the garage. In the summer we are really busy, especially at the weekends. Our garage is on the way to the 'seaside'. I don't know what the seaside is but the children who tumble out of the cars to use the toilet and buy something in the shop are always very excited. After Ed the pump attendant fills the cars with petrol the grownups come to the till and pay their money and, if mum thinks they have been good, she will buy the children some penny sweets and perhaps a bucket and spade. This is when the children get really excited. I'm never quite sure what use the painted metal things have. I'd never heard of bucket and spades before but they are very popular especially the red ones! Then their dad will normally come in yawning after a long drive. Angie will ask where they have driven from. Quite often it is from a place called the mid lands where they make cars. Every summer the whole place shuts down and people come to the sea. I always get lots of strokes especially if I'm sunning myself on the forecourt. I like summer. And I like being Garage Cat. I'm a very lucky cat.

Rosemary Lewis - 2024

A Free Lunch (The Garage)

They say there's no such thing as a free lunch. Well, there is ...

One morning many years ago, when our children were small, we decided to go for a walk along the Swindon Old Town Railway Path – the disused railway that starts from Old Town and heads west into Swindon's western suburbs. I suppose it got Beechinged. The rails were torn up, and it's been turned into a very nice, quiet footpath, feeling very rural down in its cutting. We had moved to Swindon relatively recently, and had little idea of where it went – and never thought to look it up.

Our elder daughter was about six, our younger was in a pushchair. We parked in Old Town, and set off on our walk. We walked on and on, and eventually came to where the path ended – at the remains of a bridge, where we found ourselves looking over the blocked-off end of the path, high over the road beneath, with a long view across the suburbs.

And then we asked ourselves – where will we get lunch? And how will we get back to the car? It was long before we had mobile phones, there were no shops or bus stops in sight – as far as we could see, nothing but houses. We had given no thought to either of these questions!

And then, looking over the rooftops, our 6-year-old saw a bouncy castle in the distance. She said she wanted to go on it. I said it was almost certainly in somebody's garden, probably hired for someone's birthday – we couldn't barge in on strangers. But she kept pleading, so I thought, well, we might as well go in that direction as any other. So, warning her to be ready to be disappointed, we set off to walk towards the bouncy castle.

We walked a long way, and eventually got to it – and it turned to be in the forecourt of a new garage that was having a grand opening that day. As an opening ceremony, they had this bouncy castle – and were giving out free chicken salad lunches to anyone who stopped by!

I don't like chicken, but I made an exception that day! And our daughter had a wonderful time on the bouncy castle! I can't remember how we did get home – maybe we found a bus stop, or rang for a taxi from the garage. But I always remember that day, as the day that proved there is such a thing as a free lunch.

Alan Fryer - 2024

L.W.G.

All leaves Illustrated by Julia V H Fryer

Challenge 2 - ABC

One week, it was Andrea's turn to set the theme, and she set us all the task of writing pieces in which each sentence or (for a poem) each line began with the next letter of the alphabet. Here are some of our resulting pieces.

The Chase

At last, she had reached the edge of the woods and took a minute to pause. Behind her she knew the pack were closing in fast, so she could not stop for long. Cautiously she edged out into the open and looked up at the sky. Darkness was descending and would bring with it new challenges. Every bone in her body was aching, but she needed to keep going. Failure to finish was not an option at this stage of the game. Gritting her teeth, she moved tentatively forward into the open, picking her way among the large boulders and rocks which scattered the landscape.

Heaving herself onto the top of a large pile of rocks, she scanned the horizon behind her. Ideally, she wanted to see pitch black, but there were definitely moving lights in the distance, rapidly approaching her position. Just up ahead in the opposite direction there looked to be a stone building which might offer her some cover. Knowing that the clock was ticking, she jumped down from the rocks and picked up the pace to reach the building quickly.

Lifting the latch of the old wooden door she pushed it open slowly. Mistakes made now would see her out of the game, so she was not taking any risks. Nothing moved or made a noise from behind the door. Opening it to its full capacity allowed the moonlight to brighten the room beyond. Pretty confident that this was a safe space she stepped inside. Quite quickly she realised her mistake when she heard the loud click. Reacting immediately, she dropped to the floor, rolled and fired her weapon. Sacrificing the last bit of ammunition she had might be her only chance of survival. 'Target destroyed; Target destroyed' boomed a voice. Up came the scores on the screen in front of her. Victory was hers, she had found and beaten the current champion.

Winning the game meant she had moved up the champion's board. XBOX was her passion, using the games as a release at the end of a busy day, and today she had finally beaten the current champion in one of the latest games. Yawning and stretching her stiff arms and fingers she signed out of the game for the night. Zodiac259, her call sign, fell into bed and shut her eyes, happy in the knowledge she was now a gamer to be recognised.

Andrea Cook – 2024

ABC

Andrea's task is A to Z

Big ask

Can't do it right now

Delay and procrastinate

Everyone else seems to have done it

Failed again as I just can't get it!

Get the brain into gear

Head stop your whirling

Instead think hard

Just write down anything

Keep thinking.

Let's have a break.

Make a strong cup of coffee

Nice to sit down

Only that's all I've been doing.

Perhaps a piece of chocolate to stimulate the brain

Quickly while no one is looking

Ram it in my mouth

Swallow it down

Try not to choke

Until the evidence is gone

Very satisfying.

While the brain stays blank

X rated swear words fly into the air

Yelled to the rooftops.

Zero response.

(Whew. Got away with it and I am done)

Rosemary Lewis - 2024

ABC

A bear awakes
Being hungry after so long asleep
Cave is empty though, no food around, cobwebs everywhere
Down to the river he goes
Easily catching some fish
Full and content he wanders the woods
Growling as he catches a scent
Humans are here, camping in a glade
Isn't it wonderful, says the leader of the group
Just think of the walks and stories we'll tell
Killing a deer, just for its antlers
Leaving the body, just such a waste
Morning has come
Now they are hiking some more
Oh what a fuss, a bear they have seen
Padding slowly towards them, growling and fierce, a fish in its mouth
Quite the surprise, and not what they want
Running away, seems to be the order of the day
Stopping at last, catching their breath
That was so scary but exciting as well
Until the next time, I think I will leave it for now
Vexed and annoyed, the bear stops and stares. The humans have gone, screaming in fear.
Xenia refused, makes the bear angry and sad
Yelling in frustration. His roar echoes through the woods
Zigzagging along, patrolling his woods, looking for strangers to say hello to.

Ross Kitchen - 2024

Note: Xenia - Greek for foreigner or stranger

ABC of Policing

Avidly in pursuit
Barely in their sights
Carefully chasing footprints
Determinedly forging forward
Effortlessly keeping pace
Frantically finding clues
Grandly displaying investigative powers
Hauntingly hiding in shadows
Idiotically taking the bait
Judgmentally delivering penalties
Kindly permitting suggestions
Laughingly ousting alternatives
Minutely inspecting evidence
Noticeably unafraid
Ordinarily avoiding conclusions
Purposely sniffing out lies
Questionably enforcing the law
Respectfully bowing to authority
Satisfyingly catching criminals
Suspiciously challenging tall stories
Tenaciously seeking offenders
Unbelievably tracking down criminals
Valuing legal tenacity
Wisely bowing to justice
Xenaciously* seeking solutions
Yawningly finishing every day
Zestfully starting each new case

Dona Allen - 2024

Note: Xenaciously - Full of strong desire for change and growth

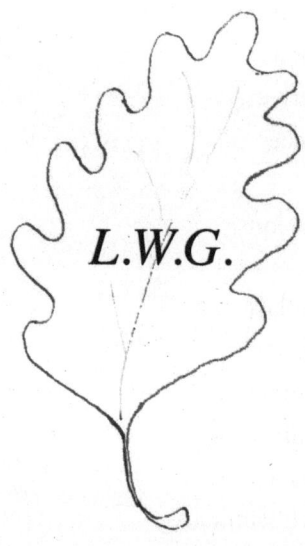

L.W.G.

Dona Allen

Hello, my name is Dona Allen and I was born in St Andrews in Scotland. With a father in the Army, a husband in the RAF and myself joining the WRAF; I have lived quite the nomadic life and am currently living in my 23rd home. I have been lucky to experience life abroad and have lived in Germany, Malaysia and Canada.

Now retired I have settled in Swindon and fill my days with Rock Choir, travelling, furniture up-cycling, crafting, writing and simply enjoying time with family and friends.

I joined the Liden Writers' Group in September 2024. Previously I had only produced the odd poem; however, more recently I find myself waking in the morning with words tumbling from me. The group has inspired me to test the waters and write my first short story (Fright & Flight), I hope you enjoy it and a small selection of my poems and stories.

Lockdown Lady

Written during the first Covid pandemic lockdown. Life changed dramatically as schools and businesses were closed. Trips out of the house were strictly limited.

My legs are getting hairy
My eyebrows need a pluck
My lips are dry and flaky
My waistline's run amuck

My hair is getting longer
I've hacked it once or twice
The grey is showing stronger
Home styling must suffice

My hands are red and sore
In water all this summer
The taps are dripping freely
I think I need a plumber

The fridge door's getting squeaky
From all the frequent use
Home cooking is the order
No dietary abuse

My garden's looking greener
Hedges neatly trimmed
The grass is oh so tidy
The weeds pulled up and binned

My home is quiet and peaceful
For weeks it's all we know
Trapped inside these four walls
There's nowhere else to go

Let's hope this virus ends real soon
And no more lives it seizes
I want to see my family
For laughter, hugs and squeezes

Dona Allen - 2020

We Honour You

One for Remembrance ...

For those who never returned home
For those who never met the love of their life
For those who never held a son or daughter in their arms
For those who never said a final farewell to their mum, dad, wife, family and
friends
For those who never saw the children grow
For those who never walked down the aisle with their daughters
For those who never fulfilled their potential
For those who never had the chance to grow old

We honour you now and forever

Dona Allen - 2024

Illustrated by Dona Allen

Without You at Christmas

This poem was written during the first Christmas after my husband died.

This Christmas morn is full of tears
Where sounds of joy should be
The house is full of emptiness
A ticking clock and me

Since you left this earthly plane
The days are long and quiet
No arms to put around me
Just sadness and disquiet

I thought I'd be ok at Christmas
I thought I had it nailed
But feelings bubble up inside
Overflowing – I think I failed

The table setting just for one
Your chair collecting dust
Your hat and gloves still in the drawer
Alone – 'I must adjust'

When living as a couple
With all the strains and strife
Little do we appreciate
The emptiness of life

I fill my days with this and that
To take away the pain
I set a smile upon my face
My love for you won't wane

I doesn't matter what I feel
It's not a time to wallow
So join the festive spirit
Don't think about tomorrow

A family day to celebrate
Of lives and love ahead
Our hearts are full of memories
Our love for you – just said

To Colin with love 💕

Dona Allen - 2020

Farmer Lee - Haydon Meadow

Inspired by the antics of 350 sheep using Haydon Meadow and the land west of Cricklade Railway. For several weeks Facebook was awash with sightings of wayward sheep. Whilst at times it was frustrating; the locals rallied around and many met neighbours for the first time - we became a 'community'.

Farmer Lee did get some sheep
To graze and earn a buck
Initially well behaved
But then they ran amuck

Breaking through fences
And a hedge or two
If they're not too careful
They'll be a pot of stew

An outing to the Tawny Owl*
For grass and not a jar
Those youthful pesky terrors
Have travelled long and far

Some tangled in the briars
Their wool caught fast and tight
To free those naughty critters
The farmer used his might

Escaping sheep did forge a route
The railway formed a track
They went through parks and gardens
Some found their own way back

Facebook was alight with tales
Of sheep both wild and free
Renamed the Mouldon Marauders
No longer the Mouldon Three

The farmer pulled his hair out
As every day they ran
We wondered why they did it
Perhaps because they can

The farmer checked his stock each day
Repairing gaps and spaces
Made by illegal walkers
Their rubbish leaving traces

They say a farmer's life is good
Out in the natural world
But thwarted by the elements
Challenges which are hurled

To work at other farms
Some very far away
Then home to catch the wayward sheep
A task he did each day

Would you ever be a farmer
Working 20 hours a day
Out in all the weather
With very little pay

The trials and tribulations
Of starting your own herd
In the middle of North Swindon
Might seem quite absurd

Good luck in your endeavours
And everything you try
We are all behind you
A great tenacious guy

Dona Allen - 2023

Sheep herded by locals and the police - ready for removal

* Tawny Owl - local public house

Our Beloved Queen Elizabeth II

My son Greg and I travelled to London to lay flowers and a copy of this poem in Green Park. We were surrounded by thousands of other mourners who were drawn to London to pay tribute to this amazing lady.

A life in quiet servitude to a nation, oh so proud
A mother to our Commonwealth, arms wrapped all around
A smile, a wave was all it took, to warm our hearts and minds
Steadfast in your love for all, reminds us to be kind

The many miles you travelled, with family at your side
The original modern woman, placed in front and not behind
The dignity you showed, through many ups and downs
Forever diplomatic, despite the many clowns

You spread your warmth across the World, from hillock down to vales
You cared when disaster hit, visiting Aberfan in Wales
You supported other countries, in times of peace and war
You brought together Nations, you could open any door

We proudly watched you celebrate your 70 years as Queen
We saw you on the balcony, a treasure to be seen
We cried with you when Philip died, a loss so profound
You showed that life continues, when family is around

Now that you have left us, we reflect upon your days
The joy that you have brought us, in many many ways
It's time to pass the baton, your time with us is past
God rest your gentle soul – our lives are at half mast

Dona Allen - 2022

Buckingham Palace - 2nd June 2022 (Queen Elizabeth's 70th Birthday Celebration)

Fright & Flight

The ticking clock echoed loudly in the hall. Time passed without event. Little did we know of the approaching doom and the presence of strangers outside.

Tucked up inside our sleeping positions we surveyed our dark and gloomy surroundings, but nothing held our attention. Could we rest? Could we sleep?

This once vibrant art deco house now lay ruined and dilapidated as if in apology to the shiny new houses surrounding it. I suppose this house will be demolished quite soon.

The murder of its long time owner and custodian, the gentle Lady Grace, had spooked the locals and nobody came near.

How we got here is a long story, far too long to explain just now. Needless to say we felt compelled to be here.

The sky was clear and full of stars, the moon peeked through the half closed curtains, shimmers of light danced gently across the floor – but not enough to chase the shadows away.

Unexpected vibrations echoed from outside and a ripple of movement swept through the room. Should we be concerned? Is it safe? Do we leave? Do we stay? At the moment we seem safe but who can be sure.

Suddenly, the door handle slowly turned and with a long screeching groan the catch on the rusty old lock was released The door haltingly creaked open destroying the peace and tranquillity of the night. The bright moonlight came screeching into our space.

Fright….

Flight….

Herding together…..

We have to leave….

As one, we dived out of the door, not sure of direction, escaping whatever threatened us. There is safety in numbers – I think.

Why are we **never** safe?

Illustrated by Dona Allen

Once more, our colony of bats seek somewhere safer to roost.

Dona Allen - 2024

The Magic Snowflake

My name is Lyla and I'm 8 years old. It's the night before Christmas and Mummy and Daddy are in their room fast asleep. My sister Vittoria (Vitt), who is 7 years old, was so excited she couldn't settle. So, careful not to wake our parents, she crept into my room and climbed in under the soft feather duvet. Vitt snuggled into me and was whispering in my ear about all the presents Santa would bring down the chimney that night. Slowly she drifted off to sleep with a smile on her face.

Why couldn't I sleep? All I could think about was the lone wolf we had seen at the zoo that morning. I had named the wolf Snowy, as his back was all grey but, he had a round soft white patch just under his chin. He seemed so lonely and he looked at me with such sad sad eyes. I wonder where his family was. Why was he by himself, especially at Christmas?

As I drifted off to sleep Vitt appeared in front of me, pulling me by the hand, 'We have to go to my friend, Jack Frost, in Lapland' she squealed. I had never heard of her friend before, but travelling to Lapland seemed fun. Maybe we would see Santa and his helpers.

As we started our journey we were surrounded by drifts of crisp white snow and tall pine trees, whose branches reached so high we couldn't see the tops of them. In front of us was a little boy, made from snowflakes, and all he was wearing was an old woollen scarf. Vitt ran up to the boy and flung her arms around him.

"Jack, Jack how wonderful to see you" she said. As if by magic the head of a lone grey wolf appeared from behind Jack.

"Hi, my name's Snowy" said the wolf. I couldn't believe it, it was the wolf from the zoo. How could Snowy be here? Dreams are such peculiar things and fantastical things can happen, I suppose.

I could see Snowy was still very sad and he hung his head low and shivered. Jack told us that Snowy had lost his family when a large crack had appeared in the ground and his mummy, daddy and brother had fallen in, lost forever.

I ran to Snowy and gave him a big hug. "I'll be your family" I said.

Snowy raised his head and replied 'If only you could stay, but this is just a dream and you'll wake up in the morning tucked up in bed'.

Jack piped up 'I have a magical snowflake and if we take it to Santa, he can grant one wish. We can ask for Snowy's family to come back home. Will you join us on our journey?' Vitt and I jumped at the chance to visit Santa.

In a blink of an eye we were outside Santa's workshop. Elves were running around filling sacks with piles of parcels that were all sorts of funny shapes and sizes. As we entered the workshop, we heard a loud 'Ho Ho Ho, what do we have here?' It was Santa, with big round red cheeks and long white fluffy whiskers and beard - just like in all the children's stories.

'Jack, you've brought some friends. Hello everyone, what can I do for you?' boomed Santa. Jack explained the story of what had happened to Snowy and his family. Santa was so saddened by the tale and gave Snowy a big hug.

'Well let me have the magical snowflake and let's see if I can help Snowy and his family' said Santa.

We all sat in a circle around Snowy, who was very scared by all the activity around him. Santa raised the magical Snowflake above his head and chanted.

'Fee Fi Fo Foam, bring Snowy's family home'.

'Fee Fi Fo Foam, bring Snowy's family home' we all joined in and kept repeating the chant.

We nearly jumped out of our skins when three loud popping noises rang out in the workshop. All the elves stopped work and stared at the wolves. Snowy's mummy, daddy and brother appeared in front of us. What a miracle! Snowy jumped up and ran circles around his family and they all rubbed noses in greeting. Snowy had his family back and he won't be alone at Christmas. We all danced around with happiness.

Merry Christmas everyone – happy dreams.

Dona Allen - 2024

Note: with help from Lyla and Vittoria

Ladies in Hong Kong

Inspired and written during an enjoyable holiday in Hong Kong with some dear friends

Hong Kong beckons, the trip begins
The houses cleaned, the rubbish binned
Glad rags on, cases ready
The car arrives, the ladies heady

Heathrow lounge, a glass of bubbly
Premier class, that's 'lovely jubbly'
Attentive staff, a few more glasses
Another wine, as the hostess passes

Planes are stacked, it takes a while
Now we're off, which brings a smile
The plane goes up, we're on our way
Night time skies to the Milky Way

We've lost a day, but do we care
We finally land, to rich spiced air
Transfer slow, but the sights amazing
The sky high buildings, lights a blazing

Dawn then cracks, we're wide awake
Eight hours difference, goodness sake
Breakfast treats, steak and dumplings
Rather that, than Halloween pumpkins

Victoria Peak, by funicular tram
Chris charged twice, it's not a scam
Dramatic skyline, sights to behold
Asian wonders, stories to be told

View from Victoria Peak

Tamar Park and Isabel's memories
Times gone by, famous Star Ferries
Night time crossing, the breeze so cool
To Harbour City, a bright lit jewel

Canton Road and high class shopping
The price of goods, our eyes a popping
Temple market, cramped and crowded
Sellers hawking and Isabel hounded

Julie's sorted, she's planned ahead
Sightseeing now, afternoon in bed
Night in the harbour, the market as well
Dinner with cocktails, diet's gone to hell

Sham Shui Po, for Dona's needs
Jade, silver and precious beads
Chris bought towels, for Sue to use
The market stirs, senses to abuse

Junking in the harbour, water calm and clear
Bouncing lights on water, stepping up a gear
A symphony of colour, beaming through the night
Played in time to music, the pulsing dancing light

To plan ahead is folly, the typhoon stopped it all
Boats stuck in the harbour, didn't move at all
A wicked turn of weather, no lucky number eight
Pier 9 is empty, determining our fate

Star Ferries

A local bus to Stanley, the number 63
Back seat on the upper deck, a better view to see
Kings Road Hong Kong, a slightly different vibe
Same double deckers, but tram lines to the side

Stanley Market small and cramped, a stones throw from the sea
The stalls were full of colour, amazing vibrancy
Prawn and apple skewers, went down just a treat
A toast to our hubbies, time to rest our feet

Saturday already, only 2 more days to go
The safe has locked our passports in, the cost to fix - Oh No!!
Shall we go or shall we stay, our visas last till May
I bet my dear old Hubby will have a word to say

Sneaker Street for Julie, for trainers she adores
Off to the Peninsula, for tea and cakes galore
Quite a high class setting, for all the girls and me
Dainty finger sarnies and Lapsang Souchong tea

Queuing for an hour, really doesn't seem too fair
Atmosphere delightful, with music in the air
Plates of goodies stacked so high, a feast to treat our eyes
Delicate patisseries, no Melton Mowbray pies

My good friends Isabel, Chris and Julie - before high tea

Then off to Ladies Market, just off Nathan Road
Gifts for all our families, our baskets might explode
Strolling pavements up and down, to find a drink or food
Empty rumbling tummies, exhaustion sets the mood

Tried to get to sleep last night, to a cacophony of sound
The guys next door were partying, smoking's not allowed
Management came up promptly, to see what it's about
Then called us to confirm, they kicked the blighters out

Delicious Kitchen, Causeway Bay, Chinese for our plate
Hot tea, beers and bowls of rice, tonight we're eating late
Chinese chatter all around, can't hear ourselves think
Tasty food for our tums, but only beer to drink

Hong Kong is so lively, the sights, the smells, the sounds
The smiling happy faces, that follow you around
They offer help when you are lost, to set you on your way
A wonderful experience, to everyone we say

Now if you choose to travel, to this far and distant land
Remember this long poem and keep the words at hand
Take all the modes of transport, with lots of sights to see
I'm happy to escort you, for a hefty tourist fee

Dona Allen - 2018

My Fair Lady (or was she?)

So gentle in her manners
Society will say
Attends the church on Sundays
Kneels down and always prays

So dainty in her bearing
White gloves are always worn
But beneath the cool exterior
Her petticoats are torn

Her bonnet at a jaunty angle
It appears somewhat askew
Propriety is demanded
Or gossip will ensue

Has she been out riding
No horse within the stable
She doesn't own a side-saddle
To ride – she is not able

Has she shunned her etiquette
To ride with Captain Cook
A military man of standing
Usually living by the book

Maybe there's attraction
We saw it at the ball
A touch of hands, a smile or two
Alone within the hall

She must watch her reputation
Her standing in the ton*
As any impropriety
Will see her standing gone

So ladies learn this lesson
Take care how you appear
It's all about decorum
You'll have nothing then to fear

Dona Allen - 2025

Note: inspired by the TV programme Bridgerton

*Ton - upper class society

Scottish Road Trip

A 900 mile trip around Scotland with a good friend. Each day I wrote a verse or two to record our amazing experience.

A drive to Bristol, to take a flight
Then onto to Callander, to spend the night
Covid strikes and dinner is cancelled
But Haggis supper is quite substantial

A quiet seat, by the river Forth
To squawking gulls, down from the North
Then off to bed, at Crags hotel
One night here and a swift farewell

A fire alarm to start our day
A quick hot shower, then on our way
Dr Finlay's home, just up the hill
The Green Welly stop - for a hearty fill

Morgan cars, an outing for fun
Attracting attention - just out for a run
Then windy roads around Loch Lubnaig *(pron. loob nick)*
Glencoe and mountains, the scenery Triassic

Around Loch Leven, with a surface like glass
Reflecting the mountains, the views first class
A visit to Elizabeth, in Kinlochleven
The local hall and it's Knit Natter season

Then on to Fort William, it's just me and you
Enjoying the lochs - 'Auch aye the noo'
Ben Nevis hotel to put up our feet
A fire alarm and beat the retreat

Loch Leven

Go west to Glenfinnan, last trip of the day
Harry Potter's viaduct, Hogwarts this way
The Jacobite rising & Bonnie Prince Charlie
A precursor to Culloden, with a strong Scottish army

Glenfinnan Monument (panoramic view)

A good night's sleep and a gentle start
A hearty breakfast, before we depart
A Benderloch visit to Chic and Linda
A cuppa and chinwag, for family we linger

Views of the loch, from the kitchen table
Stories of old and the odd Scottish fable
A stop for lunch, on our way to Loch Awe
Kilchurn Castle - a ruin we saw

Deep in the Trossachs, mountains and hills
Feeling of peace – our hearts it just fills
In the steps of our ancestors, we did tread
A visit to Oban, then back to our beds

A sleep disturbed, by deliveries and staff
Refuelling the hire car, did make us laugh
A road trip to Elgin, on the A82
The loo stops available, amazingly few

The sun it was hiding, but trying to shine
The mist round the hills, like a top hat, looked fine
Commando Memorial, stood lonely and proud
A lone piper's music, hauntingly loud

The tributes to lost ones, placed there with care
The memories of soldiers, alive in the air
Visitors and mourners, surrounding the site
Reverently appreciating, their bravery and fight

Loch Lochey and Ness, stretch all down our route
Nessie kept hidden, he's known as a beaut
Fort Augustus built after the Jacobite rising
A man in the water, somewhat surprising!

The dark peaty water, filling the locks
Attracting the visitors, who love all the 'Jocks'
St Michael's guest house, a peaceful night
A period property, a sheer delight

Walnut dressers, and old oak stairs
Real high ceilings, and chandeliers
Haddock for breakfast, with two poached eggs
Sausages, hash browns – 'Enough' she begs

The Cairngorms beckon, the whiskey trail too
Aberlour and Glenlivet, to name just two
Then onto Tomnavoulin, to Mum's place of birth
Back to her home town, returned to the earth

Gran's place of service, at old Minmore House
Grandad a farm hand, chasing the grouse
Knockando wool mill, closed for the day
Some wasted time, drove miles out the way

So back up north, to Bow Fiddle Rock
The grey windy coastline, birds they did flock
The rain not forgiving, back home in a hurry
The end of the day, saw a bowl full of curry

Next stop Lossiemouth, planes not in sight
Lining the pans, none took flight
Travelling the Cairngorms, mist drawing down
Raindrops and wipers, a mesmerising sound

Lecht and Glenross, no one at the gates
Rows of empty chairlifts, snow dictates their fate
Corgaff Castle; sitting white and bright
A star shaped wonder, 'twas really quite a sight

Up and down the hilly roads, like a game of peek-a-boo
Will the road turn left or right, 'I did'nae hae a clue'
A wee stop in Braemar town, a chip or two eat
A quick peek in the chocolate shop, and a yummy gooey treat

As we near St Andrews, with Leuchars on our right,
Fat Alberts* flew above our heads, it gave us such a fright
The next hotel is on the course, it's green with many shrubs
A game's not on the cards today, we didn't bring our clubs

A wander round St Andrews, to see a ruin or two
The streets were full of students, tourists are too few
The day was long and tiring, our eyes are sore and red
It's time to turn the car around ,and put ourselves to bed

Cathedral of St Andrews - built in 1158

A bright sunny morning, to start our final day
With fresh cut fields, and golden bales of hay
A short visit to Cupar, and Uncle Davy's shop
Cakes from the bakers, our waists will surely pop

Uncle Ray's for family lunch, their house sits on the Tay
A marvellously filling meal, what more can one say
Uncle Bill and his stories, brought family tales to life
Aunt Betty so gentle, our Queen of East Fife

A trip around the coast, memories to unfold
The homes from my childhood, sights to behold
So farewell to Bonnie Scotland, to return another day
Tomorrow we go back home, to book another stay

Dona Allen - 2021

* *Fat Alberts - affectionate RAF name given to Hercules aircraft*

The Village Hall

I sit upon a hill, my sides tall and straight
Surrounded by a picket fence and a short white metal gate
Flower borders full of colour, bees fly high all day
Well trimmed grass all around, a place where children play

Monday brings the mums and tots, having cups of tea
Tupperware full of cakes, £1 the weekly fee
Tuesday's scouts do trials and tests, to earn a badge or two
On Wednesday Knitter Natters, but now there are so few

Thursday is a busy one, with many ladies there
With rows of stalls and traders, selling all their wares
Jams and jellies, bread and rolls, even pickles take their place
Every corner filled with chatter, a noisy social space

Friday night is full of fun, it's bingo night you know
Big pens dabbing numbers, all ages have a go
Saturday is disco time, dancing on my floor
Music stops at 10 o'clock, which leaves them wanting more

Sunday is a day of rest, my insides get a clean
My floor is brushed, my windows washed, polish brings a sheen
The old door gets a drop of oil, to stop the groaning sound
The stringy mop dunked in water, swishing all around

I've seen so many people come inside my doors
I've even had the odd stray dog, with very muddy paws
I couldn't say how many, I simply can't recall
I don't have a brain you know, I'm a simple Village Hall.

Dona Allen - 2024

Illustrated by Dona Allen

The Dentist

Inspired by a recent trip to my dentist

It's not a place I like to go
It conjures up some fear
The noise and smell I loathe so much
And all that drilling gear

I brush and floss twice every day
To keep my teeth intact
Six monthly check-ups and a clean
My healthy dental pact

But it doesn't matter what I do
To keep repairs at bay
Those cheeky cavities appear
With throbbing pain all day

The appointment comes around real quick
I suppose I can't delay
Then the dentist does a pain-free fix
And sends me on my way

Illustrated by Dona Allen

A warning though, a tale of woe
You know it's not the end
The tooth is cracked, a swollen jaw
Pain drives me round the bend

Once more I sit upon the chair
The nerves and fears are back
Needles diving for my face
To fix that painful crack

Let this tale remind you
That dentists do their best
But now and then it might go wrong
So please, do not get stressed

Dona Allen - 2025

Spring

I see the thin layer of ice on the garden pond slowly melting

I see young green shoots poking their heads above the ground

I see snow and sleet turning to rain

I see warm furry boots replaced by 'Wellies' and trainers

I see fair weather walkers returning to our footpaths

I see squirrels rooting around for the remains of their winter stockpile

I see the tender shoots of the tulips forcing their way through the bark chips

I see the soft buds of the camellias thickening, promising a wondrous display

I see deer returning to the meadow, lying in their favourite spot, capturing

the brief bursts of sunshine, as it peaks through grey clouds

I feel the hope of Spring and the promise of a warm Summer

So shake off the winter blues

Take joy in the new life around you

Spring is on the way!

Dona Allen - 2025

Illustrated by Dona Allen

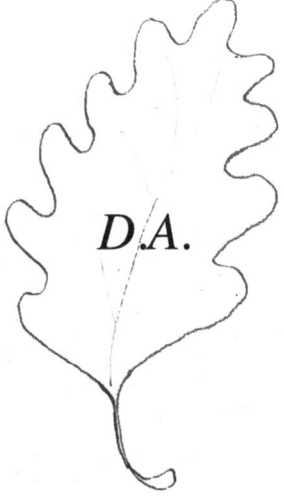

_D.A._

Irene Berridge

I was born in Alexandria, Egypt where my father was stationed and where my mother's many friends and relatives (my mother was Greek) were scattered. Fast forward thirty-five happy life years during which time we travelled quite a bit, and here I am in Swindon, where I have lived ever since.

One place that was never left out of the family travels was Symi, a tiny little island in the Dodecanese where my yiayia (granny) lived, together with cousins and uncles and aunts, and where I feel a shadow of myself drifts there permanently, dancing up and down the narrow streets and steps, greeting an old man with a donkey, waving to a child on his way to school, feeling my heart lurch as I jump into the deep blue sea and where my walks follow the tracks of thyme-scented bracken and an oregano trail.

Ever since I can remember I have wanted to be a writer. I imagined myself using a quill to write my first book as I was living in an era of inkwells and dipping pens. However, work had to come first. And so did my wonderful family. And now, mission accomplished, I can write.

The Rose

I was there waiting for him. Ben. One minute I was alone and the next I saw him emerging from a fathom of darkness in the far corner of the hall. It was his favourite entrance. 'My grand entrance,' he used to say and would waltz gracefully, swaying here and there on his way to the centre of the hall, a golden light beam following him from the ceiling. His piercing blue eyes searched until they found mine and then we were locked into each other's gaze. A gaze that was sinking into my soul, wrapping around my heart like a vine around its red fruits, pulling at feelings that had long been dead.

We were at the Golden Moon Night Spot where we had met years ago. He was wearing his blue suit and a light blue shirt. He also wore a dazzling grin; it was like sheer sunshine circulating around him. He was as I remembered him, tall, boyish, and golden tanned. His short hair surrounded his head in dark alluring waves that overlapped each other, and my heart somersaulted with the joy of seeing him again. A tear pricked the corner of my eye but I drove it away with a blink. This day was not for crying.

I was wearing my white summer dress with the scalloped neckline and the pale blue cornflowers embroidered all over. It was the one he had bought me for my birthday, and it still fitted me. Had I changed since I'd last seen him? Would he mind if I had? I wondered if he noticed.

'Shall we dance?' Ben with his captivating smile was now by my side, his steps so light that his feet barely touched the dance floor. Without a word I took his outstretched hand and right away we were enveloped in an embrace, so gentle, so serene, as we commenced a slow shuffle to the music that was playing. I closed my eyes and saw rainbows, balloons and thousands of petals falling around us. Their fragrance filled our world and I danced on in this magic setting.

'They are playing our tune.' I was breathless, exhilarated. To be in his arms again, I could not have wished for more. Our tune - *I'll Be Seeing You* - and it was Vera that was singing, just as she had long ago. We were in perfect harmony with each other.

This is right, it is how we were meant to be.

He was humming in my ear. 'I remember the music.' He held me close to him. I leant on his shoulder and could smell pines and bluebells and wild roses. We were comfortable, swaying to and fro like feathers in a gentle summer breeze. We were light on our steps, gracing the music with our movements in our memorable past.

'We were very happy,' he murmured. 'We went places did things – why we ended up at the Serpentine one day!' He pulled away from me, those deep blue eyes once again piercing into mine. His face creased to a smile at the recollection. 'We rocked ourselves silly in a clapped out rowing boat and pretended we were in choppy waters.' He was reminiscing and laughing at his memories. I laughed with him and as I looked I could see the past around us wrapping us into a happiness we once shared. And Vera's voice continued softly around us, warm and soothing.

'We were in our youth,' I tried to justify our actions.

'We paddled our feet as well, just like two-year olds,' he continued reminiscing.

'You could also mention that I raced you in the park, and that I won,' I teased.

'Ah!' He held me gently to him, laughing even more now into my hair. 'I was testing you. It was fun. We went to the Café Nous and bought some chips – oh, the taste of them, earthy and vinegary and salty – and we ate them out of newspaper.'

'We didn't have the money for fish as well.' How things have changed.

He stood back searching intently into my eyes. 'I've missed you.' His voice faltered.

He kissed me lightly on the side of my neck, as he had done so many times before. It sent fireworks through my body, explosions everywhere, pops and bangs. I trembled in his arms.

'You were my first love, Kate.' 'I know.' We were looking at each other again. His eyes were blue, azure blue. I felt myself not falling but diving into their innocence.

'And you were my first love,' I mouthed though he knew anyway. Our love had been so intense that we had never for a moment thought that it would ever end.

'You were my last love too. I will always love you Kate, always.' His eyes were still searching mine. Could he see my sadness of losing him? How futile life is sometimes.

How short.

'This is our anniversary,' I said.

'I hadn't forgotten,' he whispered. 'That is why I came. It's hard to believe so much time has flown by.'

'Have you been happy Ben?' It was important to me to know that he had been happy. I had spent so many years wondering. I hadn't searched for him. I knew where he had gone and that I couldn't reach him. Now I just wanted to know that he had been happy.

'Yes,' he answered. 'I make believe we are together – that you are there just to touch, to hold, to laugh with. It keeps me going.' His voice was relaxed. 'I'll tell you what,' he said, changing the subject suddenly, 'shall we go for a boat ride? You know, along the Embankment. It is nice and cool out now and we will see all the lights.'

The air outside was calming and smooth like velvet. We ran across the road, and then walked along the Embankment until we came to where the pleasure boats were. We didn't need to join the queue. We went straight past the crowd and as Ben stepped on the ramp he held his hand out to me. The ticket collector took my other hand to steady me down the steps and onto the boat. We found some seats facing the way we would be travelling so that we could see all the sights approaching.

'Look at the London Eye.' I pointed to him excitedly, 'that wasn't here when we met.'

'No, it wasn't,' he agreed as he looked up to it. 'If we have time, it would be good to go on it, don't you think?'

'I'd love that,' I nodded, though not sure if we would have time after our boat trip.

'Come along Kate, we still have the time,' said Ben a while later, and we were off the boat as quick as we could and hand in hand we rushed to the London Eye.

'Quick, jump on.'

It was dark by now and we travelled oh so very slowly. As we went up and up somehow it became lighter and lighter all around us, until we found ourselves cradled in a golden globe, with all of London aglow beneath us. It was immense. So many lights, so many colours, it was mesmerising. I looked at Ben and caught him studying me, wonder in his face that I too was feeling.

It was great to be here, to be with each other, to share all this on our special day.

When we reached the ground we walked along a little. He had his arm around my shoulder and the warmth of his love created tingles all over my body. We came to the bridge that we had crossed earlier. He reached over to the flower seller that was standing on the corner and picked a red rose.

'This is for you my love.' I took it and on tiptoe I planted a kiss on his lips; they were moist and warm, sweet. He is so perfect. The rose had a wonderful fresh fragrance, and I knew I would treasure it knowing that Ben had given it to me. We were coming to the end. We had to part here at the bridge. He had to go back. I had to leave as well. I had been dreading this moment.

'Let me hold you Kate.' We clung to each other. He tenderly smoothed my face, kissed my eyes, my neck. We kissed, again and again. He created chills up and down my spine. I didn't want this moment to end, and there was a hurt that was climbing up into my heart, twisting inside of me and I didn't know how I was going to bear our separation again. There was no holding him here. He had to go. 'And now I have to leave you, my darling Kate. Goodbye my love, take care.' He kissed me again, burying his face into my silver hair; we were both crying. I tasted the salt of his tears whilst mine cascaded in a waterfall down my cheek. He brushed them aside with his thumbs as he kissed me once more. Then he was drawing away from me; he held his hand out to me, to touch me one last time. His eyes were laden with sorrow. Our hands still reached for each others as he glided further and further away into the shadows. Back, back he went. He was disappearing, and I couldn't stop him. We were losing each other. I couldn't move forward, my aching heart was crushed and empty. It was a void.

'It was the war. Not many people came back. I couldn't. I'm sorry Kate.' His voice from the shadows became quieter, drifting away, falling back into a chapter of a past life. Now, not even a whisper. Ben had gone. It hadn't been his fault; it was the war.

*****

'It's all right darling, I know it's our anniversary. That's why we came isn't it? Now don't upset yourself.' The voice was David's. I opened my eyes and he was leaning over me, a look of concern in his face. Now I know where I am. We had come to London and we were celebrating. We had settled on a bench along the Embankment, watching the boats on their tours up and down the Thames. I must have dozed off.

'Let's go for a stroll before dinner,' said David.

I got up from the bench and put my arms around my husband.

'Hang on you've dropped something,' he bent to pick it up. 'Well I'll be blessed,' his voice had a tinge of surprise in it. 'I was just about to search for a flower seller.' In his hand he held a red rose.

Irene Berridge - 2015

Carlotta

Carlotta was very distressed. She had grown up chirping around the farmyard and playing with all the other chicks. Then she became an adult. Carlotta sensed she was an adult, because she now seemed to be more perceptive. Saw how things were going on around her world sphere. And without realising it, she was sinking into a very deep, depressive state.

This was due to her friends mostly. She first had this feeling when she'd gone rushing off to see Daisy a few days ago, only to find her gone. Daisy was her best friend. Same colour feathers as her. Same height. In fact, they could have hatched from the same egg, they were that identical.

"Gone?" said Carlotta when Boo-boo told her. "Gone where?"

Boo-boo shook her head. "I saw a hand reach out that night, just as they were locking us in for the day. The hand picked Daisy up and went off with her. Poor Daisy, she did kick up a fuss, but to no avail."

Carlotta must have slept right through that, as she could not remember a thing. She left Boo-boo and went off to cluck around the farmyard. Not that any good would come of that. It did however give her time to think. Though even then she came up with nothing.

Another night was upon them. And this time, Carlotta was awake. Since Daisy's disappearance, she could not sleep very well. That is how she saw a large hand reach down into their chicken coop and grab – "oh no, not Boo-boo!" – and off they went.

Morning came and Carlotta could not wait to be out in the yard. She would search for her friends. After an hour she had found very little evidence to help. She clucked a little as she made her way to the farmhouse itself. On the way she stopped. Feathers, golden speckled feathers – just like hers – were strewn on the muddy ground, lifeless, dull and dead.

"In fact," Carlotta thought, "my poor friends must be dead."

Carlotta jumped. She began to run along the farmyard, splashing mud everywhere, her wings flapping to help her along. She tried flying, but it didn't work. She rushed to the nursery where chicks were happily playing, bent down and scooped them both under her wings. Then she ran again, tried to do it silently, but her fear had built up into her chest and now she was clucking her way along the dirt track.

Out through the gates where the cars shot past, out into the lane where Lady Stephanie rode her pony, and finally, the chicken crossed the road into the wood, and she kept going until she felt the whisper of safety from the trees around. Only then did she open her wings wide and drop her beautiful yellow chicks onto the soft earth of their new surroundings.

Irene Berridge - 2024

Charlie and Joanna

Charlie stood. It was all he could do not to start jumping up and down and cheering, as he watched her spectacular approach. Big strides, hopping skipping, jumping over imaginary potholes. Joanna headed towards him, running like a five-year-old, one hand waving wildly in the air, her dark hair bouncing up and down with her movements; her other hand held onto her suitcase as it rolled behind her. He had dreamt of this moment for so long, and then here they were him standing there bemused and she just an inch away from him, her face laughing up to him. Crystal tears had rolled down her cheek as she had journeyed towards him.

His tears were within him. Drenching his heart, his ribcage felt as if it would burst and his heartache would overflow, pour onto the chequered marble flooring.

Was this the same as when they were young? When Joanna had stood in front of him, teenagers together, holiday for the last time, with their families before they went their separate ways? They'd held hands then, days of innocence, of preparing to go out into the world, become adults. Make their way as they wished. Now here they were together again, much older, perhaps much wiser, but still laughing to each other, their piercing eyes burning deep into each others' souls.

"Charlie, it's real. I'm really here with you!" The suitcase slammed to the ground as her fingers relaxed. And now her hands were waving up in the air, twirling round and round.

"Stop, you will fall!" he laughed. He had always been the practical one, had said that to her before in the past. Now she pirouetted in front of him.

Joanna laughed even more, then stopped. "And you, Charlie – turn, let me see you."

He did a turn for her. Around them people bustled to get out of the airport. Charlie and Joanna were oblivious to them. Their dream was unfolding in front of them. He wanted to hold her, to pick her up. Brush her tears gently, talk to her softly, kiss any sorrow away. Yet they were happy too, he knew. Happy to have travelled from their homes to this beautiful destination.

"We must go now." He eventually found his voice. "We must find a taxi and get to the hotel. Once we are rid of this luggage, we can find somewhere to eat, and perhaps a cool drink."

"Charlie, you will never change. Come then," and she picked up her belongings. They walked slowly to the exit of the airport. Once outside, the night air engulfed them, and they stood again, looking about them. "Roma, here we are!" called Joanna to the night, to the sky and the stars. "Here we are at long last!"

Charlie laughed out loud. "You have not changed either, Joanna, you are still impetuous."

She began to dance in the road and hummed her way up and down the paving. "Come join me!" she cried.

"No way, we must get a taxi."

It didn't take long before one drove to them and they bundled into it. They sat close to each other. Charlie put his arm around her shoulders. It felt strange after so much time apart. He slowly drew his arm back.

"Gosh we're here already!" Joanna's eyes were wide with excitement. Dancing and swaying, laughing and singing, Joanna made her way to the steps of the hotel.

"Nice room," ventured Charlie. And he walked about, examining everything. The bed was huge. "Seems that bed would take four easily," he remarked.

"Talking of which..." Joanna went to inspect it. "do we have a slight problem?"

"Not that I can see," Charlie replied.

"Well," she continued." "I am wondering what the etiquette is on two unmarried people sleeping together – albeit in an enormous bed." She looked at him, for the first time serious.

"To be honest, at least one person is married," Charlie replied, watching her carefully.

"OK," she nodded. "Perhaps we can just hold hands."

"Of course, that's exactly what I was thinking too," he said. And she was now in his arms, in that forbidden embrace which shouted to them both those countless words that only the walls were listening to.

"How I've missed you," he whispered, "How I've longed for you."

"Charlie, you promised," she whispered back feeling the pain in her chest.

"I know, my love, I know," he kissed her tenderly, then let go. "Let's change, then go."

"Shall we walk? I'd love to see a bit of our surroundings."

"Yes of course," he agreed. "We can hold hands as we go."

"Of course we can." And she grabbed him quickly.

Outside the air was not changed. They felt the breeze, bringing with it sweet scents of the roses that grew in rows along the pavement. They walked aimlessly in the comforting night, following the line of twinkling lights leading them along the strata to the fountain. When Joanna saw it she wanted to run.

"No, wait," Charlie implored her. "Wait, so that we both get there together."

And so they arrived, still holding hands, to the Trevigo fountain, whose water still trickled in layers, and splashed loudly into the bed of coins at the bottom. So much happened around this fountain. Lovers came and went, all throwing coins, and all mouthing pleas.

"I must find a coin and make a wish." Joanna was searching in her handbag desperately. "I know I have a coin at the hotel."

"We'll do this tomorrow. What coin have you got, Joanna?"

"You know, the one you gave me last time. When we came as children. Do you remember? I still have it."

He remembered only too well.

They ate outside at a tiny little bistro. They left only when the lights were being turned off one by one.

Back in their room they prepared to rest. They stopped by the bed. This was not part of their adventure. Was it a dare? Dared they get into this enormous bed together? Joanna was first to pull the bedclothes back and jumped in quickly, her gown sliding to the ground. Charlie shook his slippers off, and climbed into his side. They found each other somewhere in the middle, and immediately arms found a body to cling to. Lips sealed so many unsaid words in their immense joy of being together, and eventually, silence fell on the lovers as they slept, enveloped in each other's arms.

Irene Berridge 2024

A Ghost Story

Marion peered out of the window. She could just see the car through the cloud of dust that it created along the dirt track that her parents proudly called a driveway. When it rained the track didn't emit dust like today; when it rained their car edged carefully along, or it sank into the pools of water that abounded here and there. If Marion was riding in the car she could not wait for it to stop and let her out. She'd run off and expend her energy in the massive pools and potholes that resulted.

Today it was not raining. It had not rained for some days. Marion waited until the car had fully disappeared down the lane and then ran to the back door, threw it wide open and said, "You can come in now, they're gone." A girl entered the kitchen. Her hair had been blown by the wind and wisps were hiding her pink cheeks. With one hand she swished them away while her eyes travelled around the surroundings.

"Did you wait long?" Marion asked.

"No, not really," the girl replied, still scrutinizing the room. "What shall we do today?" the girl asked.

"Whatever you want," Marion replied. "Let's go to the playroom."

They both ran out of the kitchen, and up the stairs. Marion was way ahead of her friend. When Livvy eventually caught up with her, they both used their strength to push the large solid door of the playroom, open. The room was full of toys. A large chest was pushed into the far corner and Livvy ran excitedly to explore. She edged the top up, and her eyes filled with pleasure, as she stared into its contents. Elegant gowns, coats, hats, bags, and glistening jewellery.

"Shall we dress up?" asked Livvy, lifting a dazzling green silk gown, totally covered in sequins. "Which of these clothes did your ghosts wear?" she asked.

Marion had told her of their ghosts when they had met a few days before in the woods. Livvy was awed at first, but when she had gone home for her tea that day, her mother had laughed when she heard the story. "Your new friend sounds to be quite a story teller, darling!"

Livvy's mother always was right in everything she had told her, and Livvy decided that perhaps it had been a story to while away the afternoon. After all, as Livvy's mother said, ghosts only crop up in books, a bit of fun.

Marion looked over her shoulder now, as she crouched at the wooden chest. "Oh, I don't know," she shrugged. "I think they've worn pretty much all of these at some time in the past."

"Wow!" cried Livvy. "I like this one." She pulled out a pale blue long gown, complete with its flowing train.

"That used to be Great-grandmother Sheba's," Marion remarked. "There's a picture of her wearing it in the hallway."

Livvy was not bothered. She rolled up her sleeves and began to drape the soft silk dress around her. "I love it!" She tried walking carefully not to trip over the abundance of material at her feet. "Where do you have a mirror?"

Marion looked up quickly. "Oh," she said, "there's one in my parents' room, but I'm not allowed in there."

"How about me? I can go."

"There's no ghosts in there."

Livvy waddled towards the door, lifting as much sequinned material as she could.

"Which way?"

"Right down there, the green door."

At the green door, Livvy stopped. She looked about her, but she was alone. "Marion, come on!" she called.

But Marion would not come out of the playroom. Livvy turned to the green door. She carefully took the golden door handle in her hand, pushed hard, and entered.

The room was in darkness. The curtains had been drawn. A strange sweet smell was filling the air about her. She breathed in, and after a few seconds began to feel quite faint-headed. Then she saw the mirror, edged towards it, and stood directly in front. "I love it, I love it," she managed to say, still feeling dizzy.

"How about this?" Marion had come up into the room and was stealthily squeezing herself by Livvy's side. Livvy looked up, then jumped. What was going on? She looked at her sides, to Marion in a bright red gown. She looked in the mirror – and then she fainted.

When Livvy opened her eyes next, she was lying on the carpeted flooring in the hallway. "Where am I? What happened?"

Marion was looking down at her. She was still wearing the red gown. "You fainted. I dragged you out."

"What's that smell? You know, what I smelt in your parents' bedroom?"

"Oh, that," said Marion, dismissively.

"Yes," said Livvy. "It was very sweet and my head went funny."

"It is something my mother uses. Ghosts like it, you know."
"No, I don't know. And now I remember what happened. You lost your head."

"Are you afraid?"

"No, not now your head is back. But you had lost it."

"It's a spell. We're looking for a way to break it. But so far we have not found one. Do you know how I feel when I can't see my head? Really bad."

"Well, do you know how I feel right now?" Livvy stood up. "I want to go home". With that she picked up her gown from around her and ran as fast as she could to the door, out into the damp air, and down the stone steps.

Marion was at the window again, watching. Livvy was nearly halfway down the track by that pothole. Marion at the window stared on; her eyes had gone yellow, piercing, so intense they were nearly popping out. Livvy had reached the pothole. She stopped, then a strange thing happened. She began to disappear. Marion watched, her eyes were gradually turning to brown again, and the pothole, it was surrounded by a beautiful pale blue gown, now crumpled to the ground, and whose sequins were sparkling in the light of the moon.

Irene Berridge - 2024

Anna and Cristiano

Anna watched her mother carefully. It was her mother, Maria, who had asked her to watch carefully. Not her choice at all. Her mother's gaze was not directed to Anna but fixed on the job on hand. Crystal blobs dropped periodically from her brow and from where she sat Anna could not see if in fact they were dropping into the bowl. Maria was absorbed with concentration. She had to get this right to impress her daughter.

Anna could only think that her mother had been beating those poor eggs forever. It was because she believed in the old school, her mother would tell her during a well earned rest period for her arm. Just like her yiayia Eleni, and her aunt Dina, they believed in the old ways of cooking too.

Maria was about to add the milk. Anna waited for her cue. First the eggs and sugar, then the milk and then, on cue, Anna was to add her teaspoon of vanilla. Whilst she was in this situation of waiting for something to happen, Anna rolled her eyes upwards. She'd seen others doing this when they were bored. Anna was bored. What could possibly be the use of knowing how to make a perfect custard.

'I said now, Anna. The spoon. The vanilla.'

She jumped, almost spilling the contents. 'There mama, now can I go out.'

'Anna, you haven't learnt it all yet,' her mother's voice was sharp. She knew that sound. To defy would be insane. It was so unjust. She wanted to play. She wanted to be with Christiano, somewhere in the field where he was repairing fencing.

'Mama, the vanilla is added, and everything looks perfect.' Anna persisted avoiding eye contact. The door was not too far from her, open and inviting, and yet it seemed so far away.

'How can you ever think it's done?' Maria was annoyed now. She had hoped her daughter would show an ounce of interest in at least part of the goings on. Her daughter stared into the bowl where a creamy orangey mess was being beaten. This was going to be custard? That was all that the child could see.

'You have to pay attention,' began Maria again 'If you are to be married you have to learn these things. To please your husband, your children. Now stop fidgeting and pay more attention. Look at what I am doing child.'

Anna could not tell her mother the truth. The one she wanted to marry did not really like custard. She had already told him about the lesson she was in for and she knew he would find no pleasure in having a bowl placed in front of him. They'd sat facing each other in the barn, surrounded by pecking chickens, and baaing lambs. Christiano had laughed when Anna told him. It was the way she had looked, her face so serious, her lips red like fire. He wanted to scoop the child up in his arms and tell her not to worry about it, everything would be fine, but he didn't dare. His aunt would have had something to say about it.

'Anna,' he said gently, 'you must go for your lesson. Who knows, one day you may have a suitor who loves custard.' She had not noticed how detached his voice had sounded. Anna could only think of being there, with Christiano. As for food. Her thoughts did not stretch that far. Her heart seemed to be at bursting point. Always had been when she was with Christiano. Even when she was smaller than now, her first steps had been to walk into Christiano's strong arms. He had picked her up when she fell, dried her eyes when she cried, put plasters on her grazed knees. It was only right that she should marry him. He would have somebody to cook for him, dolmathes, and salads and she would have someone to cook a custard for her the way she liked it, the way her mother made it.

Of course, Anna could not remember her baby days. These had been recounted to her time and time again by all the aunties, and her yiayia, and even her mother had told the stories often. 'I have never worried while you were at school. I knew Christiano would take care of you.'

And now this. Watching custard being made. Greek custard. In case, just in case, one day a boy would come banging on their door, knock it down even with brute force and immense urgency, and once this unknown knight had set eyes on her, he would scoop her in his arms, prop her on his white steed, climb on behind her and they would ride off into the unknown world that beckoned, and there they would build their nest and start their fairytale life together.

'Mama,' she ventured carefully, 'I am going to marry Christiano. I have not told you before, but now I have to. I have spoken to him about custard and he says he doesn't like it, or any other type of sweet things. He likes dolmathes. And anyway,' she dared to utter, 'I shall have a cook when I marry. I shall have the cook make dolmathes for Christiano, and custard for me. There is no need for me to know all this,' she waved her hands around the bowl. 'Now can I go?'

Maria was defeated. She waved her hand to her daughter. There was food to prepare. Thomas would be home soon.

Irene Berridge - 2025

A Day at the Market

Did I tell you that the real fun of my holidays abroad is not the sitting on a sunbed under an umbrella on a crowded sandy beach with a glass of something in my hand? The real fun is exploring my surroundings and integrating with the local community.

When I know I am going on holiday with Lil, anticipation of what lies ahead grabs me by the arms and twirls me several times in the air before I am lowered gently back onto terraferma. Such is the thrill of the unknown. Our holidays together are not planned so much as to where we shall go or what we shall do. Our holidays are always like an unfolding mystery tour. We each take an alternate day and offer an adventure resulting in making it really something to look forward to and cutting out an awful lot of time spent on haggling.

One year we were staying in the main town of a Greek island which has a wonderful street market once a week that stretches a mile or so, and each inch of that area is generally packed with everything that you could possibly wish to purchase. Primarily it is a food market though you can still purchase haberdashery items, plumbing materials, and no end of other household goods when you weave in and out of the maze of stalls. Diversity is the key. For our adventure that day I chose we go to market. I dare anybody to laugh on this decision. Remember every day is an adventure, so why not at a market?

Upon arrival we made our way to our first love of any market offerings, the vegetables and fruit, where art and design go hand in hand to lure the buyers. I spent time looking at the wonderful display - peppers, such vibrant reds and greens, yellows and oranges. Then there were onions all stacked up and arranged so gracefully, who would not buy them? Then also there were the aubergines, deep shiny purple skins, and next came the large beef tomatoes. My heart lurched when I saw them. They had been arranged one on top of another in the shape of a giant heart. I smelt their freshness then put my hand out to feel for a heartbeat. 'So beautiful,' I said to Lil.

'Yes very beautiful,' came a Greek voice close to my ear which made me jump. Lil does not stand so near to my ear, and she definitely does not speak Greek.

I looked to my side and there was this man. He was sort of tallish. A dusty grey jacket covered a once white shirt, and his matt of snowy hair was topped by a funny sort of trilby hat. Around his arm was a still empty faux leather shopping bag. I edged away a bit to put space between us.

'They are beautiful,' I repeated with a flicker of a smile pointing to the tomatoes.

'Yes,' he nodded his head. 'Will you marry me?'

Now that made me jump. I thought of St Valentine and wondered if that is how love should be - meet, smile, get married, etc., etc. I looked again at the man. He was not actually smiling, rather an anxious look in his eyes. They were imploring. Did he really want me to answer. I looked about for Lil. I could see her tell-tale white sunhat bouncing up and down as she strolled further from me in the crowd. Then I looked again at the man. I turned then to the tomatoes.

What would they do in a situation like this? Would that large heart really pound a rhythm? There was no inspiration forthcoming from the tomatoes nor anything else in my immediate surroundings.

'No, I can't,' I decided to say to him in Greek. I felt foolish answering such an outlandish question.

'Please can you marry me? I have no wife. I have a farm.' I was walking away now, in the direction of the bobbing white sunhat, but he was there matching my every step.

'Well,' I tried to sound firm and diplomatic, 'the thing is I have a husband, and two children, and a dog. And we have birds in the garden and sometimes cats.' I tried to show him how the situation he had created was really quite futile. Lil was there now right by me, and I blurted out 'This man wants to marry me, he has a farm.' I felt like a naughty child about to be reprimanded by her mother.

Lil looked at me and then at the man. 'Go away,' she said uncharitably to him. 'She's already married. Now be a good man and finish your shopping and then go home.' I felt sorry for the man, he must be very, very lonely I thought.

'I will take you for a coffee, a tea, a meal. Come to my farm, I have a cow and some sheep. I make feta cheese.' He really wanted to impress me, his hand pointing the way beyond. 'I make cheese good. You dig potatoes. Like this here look.' He went to the next stall and picked up some great looking potatoes, I could almost taste them baked. At the same time, that's when my moment of flattery evaporated, stabbed, shattered. 'You dig potatoes' the man had said. Me. An invisible arrow had put paid to my vanity. My head whirled, filled now with visions of wellies, muck, spades and rows of potatoes swaying to me and pleading 'me next, me next.' Behind him, a stall holder was beckoning me. I dipped my head under the man's outstretched arm and crossed over. Not another proposal surely.

'Quick,' he said. 'Here take this,' he held a pair of blue rubber gloves. 'You put on now, you take, quick. Go.'

This wasn't real. Lil was still with my suitor. I was now donning gloves, but for what? 'Quick under here,' and that is when I realised I had to go under the trellised tables and crawl along to make my escape. From the man who wanted me to marry him and dig his potatoes on his farm. The decision had been made for me. I began my journey.

Irene Berridge - 2025

Lillian and Howard

The man behind the desk was writing. Smartly dressed in a dark suit, nice hands, thick brown hair. He looked up as he heard them enter. He hesitated for a moment, taken aback. Lillian Davis caught her breath as she was ushered in. She walked slowly towards where he was, her blue eyes showing their recognition. Their eyes locked.

They had met before in another world. His grey eyes widened. He knew her from somewhere. How she had smiled just then, the way she was looking at him, she had done that before. He got to his feet slowly, tall, just as she knew him, their eyes still tangled up with each other, their minds rushing through memories, days before now. Lillian spent a moment longer mesmerised. Her head was dazed, a thousand and one butterflies flying round and round in her stomach, and then snapped out briefly to place her hand in his. He had a firm handshake. She knew he would. He had held her hand once before when she had laughingly told him that he could only touch her fingers, and he had, softly, warmly, yet firmly.

'I hope they are making you welcome,' that same voice with that slight lilt of Derbyshire in it, talking to her again.

'Yes thank you Mr. Hawkins.'

'Please Lillian, call me Howard, everybody does.'

'Howard,' almost a whisper, 'Yes thank you. They are.' His eyes had still not left her face, her features were as he knew them. Fair hair that fell down to her shoulders, cheeks, brows, lips. How he had wanted to kiss her, to touch her lips. Her deep blue eyes were now smiling at him, a faint pink colour entering her complexion. She was remembering that time; he had phoned her later and apologised for not saying goodbye. That time in her life had been so special. And then he had gone.

Josie, who was standing to the side, was not sure what was going on. 'Shall we go?' she ventured, feeling that she was intruding on something incomprehensible. Lillian was back to the present, in his office. He let her hand go slowly. She withdrew unwillingly, the warmth of his touch travelling through her fingers and dancing somewhere in between her ribs where there was now a mixture of feelings beginning to form. Where had those years gone and why had it been such a futile journey?

'Enjoy yourself,' he said still standing, watching as she went out, his eyes turning melancholy.

When they left Howard sat down. He felt in his pocket for his wallet, drew it out, felt inside where he kept one or two credit cards and inched a piece of card out.

He stared at it for a long time. Flashes of memory overtook him. What had happened that day when he had left so abruptly? The picture he was holding was almost speaking to him, confirming how things had turned out, of the events that had torn them apart.

He held his head, a feeling of despair beginning to creep into him.

Outside, Josie glanced again at the new employee. She was still pink. Had something happened in there or was she imagining things?

'That was the big boss, then,' Lillian tried to hide her confusion, to steady her voice.

'Yes,' Josie replied. 'Not married. Real gentleman. Rumour has it something sad happened in his past.' Josie's voice had turned to a whisper. Lillian did not notice. Her mind had travelled back to long ago.

Josie continued the induction process. She was pleased to complete this without any further incidents, so to speak. She threw several looks at Lillian as they progressed, but whatever had happened in Howard's office seemed to have now gone. Perhaps she had imagined it.

When they left that evening, Lillian already had her mind on what she had to do at home - look up that picture. How had she not realised where she would be working? Something was not quite right with what had transpired today.

In between buttered toast, tea, and fussing Dude, the cat, she found what she was looking for. There he was smiling into the camera. Twenty years ago. She looked closely. It definitely was him. She searched at the bottom, where the names of all the students were printed clearly, row by row - Howard Hawkins was not mentioned. The man in the office today was the same person as in this picture. He had even recognised her. Yet the photograph listed him as she had known him, Stephen Rowlings.

****

They had gone home from college together that day. They'd caught the bus and then had a mile walk to do to get to where Sophie lived.

'Why are you here?' Sophie had asked him the day after he had come to live with them. She had already been told by her father why, she just wanted him to tell her.

71

His circumstances had been very frail, very shrouded. His parents, together with his two younger brothers had gone away and left him. Stephen could not find any other words to explain the situation. They had left a note for him with a small sum of money.

'Look after yourself. We are sure you will do well. We are asking the Dawkins to take care of you. May take a month.' It had been signed Dad. No sentiment lost there, yet Stephen was not altogether shocked about this. They had often gone off and left him, mostly without informative notes. This time it seemed final. When Gerald Dawkins came to collect him it was almost a month to the day that his family had left. He had a small bag ready and they made the trip across the town to what was to be his new home. The Dawkins lived in the outskirts of town in a large house. They had a beautiful daughter, Sophie.

'My family took off,' Stephen replied simply without feeling. Their steps crunched on the sun-dried grass. Sophie looked at him. She was feeling sorry for him, but his face showed no trace of sadness.

'Do you care?' another question.

'Not really,' he replied, brushing the grass as they walked along. 'Do you mind me being here?'

Sophie thought for a moment. 'Not so much now. I thought you would be dull, a bore, but you are quite cute.' She pushed him playfully and ran ahead. When she reached the Old Barn, a dilapidated building which offered shelter from the heat, she stopped and took her jacket off.

Stephen chased after her and found her hiding behind the tractor, her yellow dress silhouetting her young figure. They seemed to laugh at nothing much and yet at everything. Now they chased about the golden corn heads - they felt like children again.

'Did you play in fields back home?'

'Not really, I can't recall going to a field. In fact I can't recall playing.'

'What did you do then?' He had got used to the insatiable questions that she asked.

'I used my computer. I had quite a lot to do.'

'Such as,' Sophie had stopped running around and had fixed her blue eyes on him.

'I was trying to make money,' Stephen admitted to her.

'Are you joking?'

'No, I did make some money. It has been put away.' His grey eyes now serious daring her to ask any more. Slowly Sophie turned back to retrieve her jacket in the barn.

'We must go, mother will be wondering what has happened to me.' They picked their books up and continued the rest of the journey in silence.

*****

'I'd like you to take a walk with me.' Gerald Dawkins was speaking to Stephen.

They had finished supper and Ellen Dawkins had gone into the lounge. Sophie took herself upstairs to get on with her college work.

Gerald Dawkins led the way down the slipway that led to the main road. The sun was just beginning to sink gracefully behind the Molten Hills, and around them the birds were whistling and chirping away in this calm summer evening. When they reached the Old Barn, Gerald Dawkins stopped abruptly and turned to face Stephen.

'What were you doing here with my daughter this afternoon?'

Stephen saw anger written all over his face. 'We were walking home from college, Sir.'

'What did you have to stop here for? You have no right.' Gerald Dawkins was indeed angry.

Stephen was confused. He could not see what was wrong. 'Sir we stopped here to get out of the heat for a bit,' Stephen said. Suddenly Dawkins grabbed Stephen by his collar and his right fist landed straight into his face. He hit him again, Stephen tried to back away, but he could not free himself. He wrenched but the older man held fast onto him, hitting him again and again. Then he let him go, and he fell to the ground.

'Keep away from my daughter. Get out of my house. You are no longer welcome.' Dawkins turned and walked back towards the house.

Stephen ached all over. His face, his stomach, his arms. He eased his shirt off and used it to clean some of the blood that was pouring off his face. He could not understand what caused Gerald Dawkins to act like that. He was so confused and for the first time in a long while he felt really saddened. He had no one to turn to, no one to give him an explanation.

It was past midnight when Stephen went up the small hill to the house. He let himself in through the back door, went up to his room, threw his belongings into his holdall and went out again into the night.

Five years on, and now a young man of twenty-three, armed with his degree that he had worked so hard for, Stephen was planning the next stage of his life. He needed his birth certificate amongst other things. He logged on to the Internet and filled in the details that were required. It took seven days to arrive. When he opened the letter he stared at it in disbelief. At first he thought there was a mistake. He went to the beach and sat down on the soft sand that evening, thinking.

*****

The next day Howard sent for Lillian. There was much to catch up on and he knew that the sooner they talked the easier things would be for them.

'Would you care to go to dinner tonight with me? I feel we need to talk, don't you?'

'Thank you Howard, that will be fine.' Lillian still felt that strange feeling in her stomach when she talked to him. He had always had that effect on her.

In the restaurant they sat across to each other. Lillian could see now that Howard was not at ease at all. 'I owe you an explanation,' he began. And he told her slowly how things had been.

'But you changed your name.'

'Yes I did. This is difficult Lillian, because on getting an original birth certificate I found that my name in fact was Dawkins. Your father had registered me. I presume I was with my 'parents' because I was my mother's and your father's son. Hence why they went away and left me, and how I found myself in your house. We are brother and sister, so to speak. We could never have been lovers.' Howard's voice was tormented with sadness.

'Howard, my dear, have you not wondered why I have changed my name? I too obtained my birth certificate. They were never my parents. I was adopted at birth.'

They both gazed at each other, and slowly reached out for each other across the table. Both were showing crystal drops falling slowly. They were sad, and glad, and gladder drops.

Irene Berridge - 2025

74

My Favourite Room

This has to be the conservatory. It was built approximately 20 years ago and is the lightest room in the house. It is also the most peaceful room. Originally we (my husband and I) decided that we would have this room as a quiet room for reading and sewing and watching the garden grow – no TV.

The quietness in those days was transformed as mayhem as my two boys used it as a games room, flying all sort of objects around it, playing pool, vrooming cars and even sleeping in it with their cousin as a treat.

For my part I had friends come along to discuss knitting and sewing and to learn Greek, and we also had countless parties. I cannot believe the amount of people that used to come just to squash around and laugh and eat and socialise.

The room looks out onto the garden. The garden has had many facelifts in its time and now is growing for us vegetables and fruit and flowers. There is a lot of colour out there. The most enjoyable time we have is when we are sitting having our meals and we can then watch the multitude of birds that come to balance themselves on the bird-feeder in order to eat a few grains or to walk about the small water tray and splash about in the water. As well as birds we have the squirrel who has discovered free food and is there twice a day. If the food is not available he jumps on to the roof of the conservatory so all we can see is his big fluffy tail trailing down. He runs around the skirting, then jumps onto the fence, jumps on to the clothes line, twirls around, jumps onto the pear tree and then transfers himself into the large oak tree to hide.

In the winter the conservatory is really spectacular with the white snow overhead. We look out to a blanket of pure white interrupted only by the wafer thin tracks of birds footprints as they walk daintily pecking away at this white haven.

Irene Berridge 2025

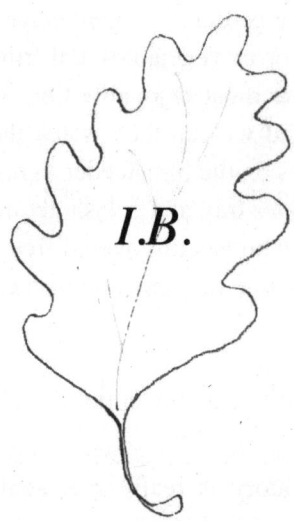

I.B.

Andrea Cook

Hello, my name is Andrea and I have been part of the Liden Writing Group since September 2022.

I have always enjoyed reading and writing and English was my favourite subject at school. Over the years, more so in my adult life, I have dabbled with poetry, writing pieces here and there for birthdays and other celebrations, and have even attempted writing a novel, which is probably sitting in my attic somewhere. When I went along for my first session with the LWG (Liden Writer's Group) I was extremely nervous about reading out one of my poems (*The Old Oak Tree*) as they had only been heard amongst family and friends. However, the group were so welcoming I felt brave enough to read it out and have not looked back since.

I hope you enjoying reading the selection of poems and the short story I have chosen for this book. I have given a brief note about each choice to give you a little background information as to why it was written.

In my spare time I like to visit National Trust properties or similar places. I love old buildings and exploring beautiful gardens. The picture below was taken at Snowshill Manor near Broadway.

The Old Oak Tree

As mentioned in my introduction, this was the first poem I read out to the LWG.

As the autumn leaves fall softly down
The old oak tree begins to frown
The coat he has nurtured throughout the year
Is slowly starting to disappear
The wind shakes his boughs and more leaves drop
'Oh no' he cries 'I'm going to lose the lot'
Then through the autumn mist he hears noises
The laughter and squeals of children's voices
They are running so fast in their bright red wellies
Kicking up his leaves and then rolling on their bellies
Oh! what fun they are having on his copper-coloured carpet
He is starting to feel less downhearted
The children have had their fun, but before they leave
They hold hands around his trunk and give him a squeeze
The old oak tree is happier now
And as Autumn takes hold, he gives it a bow

Andrea Cook – 2022

Garden Envy

We chose 3 words at random from a jar: Jealousy, Chaotic, Methodical, and had to produce a piece of writing using all three if possible.

A flash of jealousy struck as I took in the stunning scene
Of a perfect country garden, so pretty and serene
Mine is more chaotic, with planting here and there
Flowers and shrubs thrown in where any soil is spare
I have no single-coloured border, or an area for bees
But I have a pond with lots of frogs and an ornamental tree
I stumble on a summerhouse furnished with cushions and patterned throws
My brown shed has cobwebs and, in the corners, mushrooms grow
I came across a statue made of pure white marble
At the intricate detail and carving I can only marvel
I have funny gnomes, with pointy coloured hats
And my lovely Stanley, an ancient concrete cat!
I could be more methodical, but I am really not a fan
I'd rather plant things randomly than stick to any plan
But it's given me inspiration, so will buy a plant or two
And start a little border full of flowers in shades of blue.

Andrea Cook – 2024

79

Christmas Traditions

Christmas day will be here soon
Time for buying special gifts and food.
Office parties and Christmas jumpers
Holly and mistletoe sold in bunches.
Writing cards and checking lists
Making sure that no one is missed.
Choosing a tree be it real or fake
Gingerbread and stollen ready to bake.
Brass bands and carol singers bring festive cheer
Mulled wine and cider or lots of cold beer.
Remembering loved ones both present and past
By laying a wreath or raising a glass.
Papers and bows and personalised tags
Everything going in festive bags.
A trip to the panto to boo at the baddie
A cheer for Prince Charming who is looking quite dandy.
Stockings are hung at the end of the bed
Carrots left out so the reindeer are fed.
Prancer and Dancer, Donner and Blitzen, Dasher and Comet, Cupid and
Vixen.
Santa and Rudolph are soon on their way
Soaring through the sky in their magical sleigh.
Christmas Day has arrived and all through the night
Snow has been falling and all is white.
Christmas pyjamas all cosy and warm
Opening stockings in bed first thing in the morn.
A glass of sherry whilst the turkey is cooking
Time for another when no one is looking.
The table is set and candles are lit.
It is time for all the family to sit.
Parsnips and sprouts, roasties not fries
Xmas pudding and custard or just a mince pie.
Elf, White Christmas and Scrooge on the telly
Watching the King with a very full belly.
A game of 'Who am I', 'Go Fish' or 'Charades'

Granddad eager to use his new cards.
Out comes the port, the crisps and the nibbles
Then the curtains are drawn as the daylight dwindles.
Time for tea and out comes more food
To not have a plate full would be very rude.
Gammon, pork pie, crackers and cheese
Trifle or yule log, can I have some cream please.
Then soon Christmas Day draws to an end
Only 364 sleeps till you do it again.

Andrea Cook – 2022

Ghost Walk

We had to write something for Halloween. I was inspired by 'The Lanes' in Brighton, a place I really enjoy visiting. The picture was drawn by my granddaughter when she was 5.

I had not meant to scare her, I just wanted to talk
Is that not the point when you are on a ghost walk
To hear tales of the ghouls that haunt these lanes
Of the woman in white and the boy who was slain
To huddle together as the stories unfold
Shivering through fright and not from the cold
I have to admit I think it quite funny
That people love to be scared and pay good money
To walk down the lanes in the dead of night
Hoping to see ghosts and to get a big fright
The girl seemed different, though I know not why
But there was a look of despair behind her eyes
Someone screamed and the walkers all laughed
As a young lad shouted "I felt a cold, cold draft
It went round my neck like a hand squeezing tight"
Then I saw him wink to his mate on the right!
I would deal with him later, it might be fun
His feet won't touch the ground as he tries to run
It was then we all heard her, sobbing softly at first
Then it grew louder and steadily worse
A wailing so haunting it chilled every bone
The sound of the lost, the sad and alone
It was then I realised how stupid was I
To have missed the signs in those sad, sad eyes
She was new to this world of the in-between
Where some stay hidden, but others are seen
I put an arm round her shoulder and she looked up in fright

I smiled at her gently and held her tight
As the sobbing subsided, I whispered "You will find your way
But this isn't a place for a young girl to stay".
I took her to where she would find the light
Where she wouldn't be bound by the darkness of night
And as for me, well I have some haunting to do
A young man's neck to squeeze till his skin turns blue!

Andrea Cook – 2023

Freedom

I am not sure where the inspiration came for this poem, it is a slightly darker one for me and started off in one place, but ended up somewhere else.

I often think as I run through the gate and over the wall
Across the fields of grass to where the trees stand tall
If I were a bird, what would I be?
An eagle so large for all to see
Or the smallest of birds, perhaps a wren
Who could hide away from the gaze of men!
I reach the trees and sit and listen
Knowing as always, I am very well hidden
Up here I can breathe and feel my body relax
No longer on alert and watching my back
The rustling leaves lull me to sleep
Till I'm woken by a noise and take a peep
A stag stands proud at the edge of the wood
Surveying the beauty of his neighbourhood
Suddenly, he bolts at speed
Paying the tallest of hedges no heed
Over he leaps with room to spare
Disappearing into the air
I head back down the way I came
And hear that voice shouting my name
Trouble is brewing, I've been gone too long
I'm always doing something wrong
I'll be punished I know with a kick or a punch
And sent to my room without any lunch
I should pack my bag and go on the run
But I need to stay to protect my mum
Why she stays I don't understand
It seems she prefers the back of his hand

'One day, he will go too far, we'll be free"
Whispers my mum as I rest on her knee
A truer word she never had said
As two days later to heaven we sped!
The eagle soars above the trees
His wings flutter gently in the breeze
And down below in the forest glen
Flits an almost hidden little wren

Andrea Cook – 2023

Just Let Me Sleep

I go through periods when I just cannot sleep and this poem was written after one particularly bad night.

Oh please, please let me sleep
For an hour, a night a day or a week
Conversations I've had, lists and poems fill my head
Not what you want when going to bed
Oh please, please let me sleep
I feel so tired I want to weep
All those thoughts just whirling round
And now my head has begun to pound
I've counted sheep, but that got boring
And to top it all my husband's snoring
Oh please, please let me sleep
I open my eyes and at the clock I peep
It's 1pm still the middle of the night
All those hours to go before it gets light
I'll turn the radio on, some music perhaps
Will calm down my brain and help me relax
I want to get up and have a nice cup of tea
But then I'll be constantly up wanting a wee
Oh, please, please let me sleep
I'll try one more time before I admit defeat
I pull up the duvet and put on my eye mask
Hoping and praying I will sleep at last
Then slowly but surely, I drift away
With only 1 hour to go till the start of my day
I will get through the hours and try again tonight
And hope sleep comes without such a fight

Andrea Cook – 2023

Despair

A moment in time...

The lights growing dim
I'm not going to win
I can no longer cope
There is no hope
My heavy head
Feels like lead
I need some quiet
From life's riot
Help, I cry!
No one bats an eye
At the cliff edge I stare
If I jumped who would care
Just one final step
Then I'll take my last breath
I feel a hand in mine
You arrived just in time
Stop! Think!
Step back from the brink
Choose life not death
Find the strength
The storm we will weather
We are in this together
A glimmer of hope
Perhaps I can cope
Through the dim
I see light I want to fight!

Andrea Cook – 2024

Welford Park

I was inspired to write this poem after a visit to Welford Park to see the snowdrops. If you live locally, it is definitely worth a visit.

A visit to Welford Park is a must at a particular time of year
It will brighten up the dullest day and fill you full of cheer
A special little flower is in bloom which you wouldn't want to miss
And don't forget your camera as you will definitely want some pics.
As you wander along the woodland path the River Lambourn rushes by
And a patch of yellow aconites open up towards the sky.
As the sun hits the crystal clear water it sparkles and shimmers
Making its bed of rock and stone look like gold as it glimmers.
As you cross the old wooden bridge to reach the other side
You might see a fluffle of rabbits' scatter as they run to hide.
And then stretching out before you is a display of pure delight
Snowdrops as far as the eye can see, create a stunning carpet of white.
High up in the canopy mistletoe clings to the top of the trees
Whilst all along the river bank, bamboo rustles in the breeze.
And there amongst the Dogwood with its stems of striking red
Sits a stunning cheetah sculpture with a perfectly poised head
It is the home of the 'Great British Bake 'and in the marquee where it all
takes place.
You can now enjoy a large pot of tea and a tasty slice of cake.
Whilst peering down majestically over the old stone garden wall
Stand a family of rather ornate giraffes their necks so slender and tall.
You can purchase a snowdrop to plant at home and have a piece of Welford
all of your own.
And as you bid your farewell to its stunning display
You will always remember this special day

Andrea Cook – 2023

Welford Park, Newbury

The Ruin

On a night when I could not sleep, the bones of a story appeared and this was the end result.

The night sky was the blackest she had seen. Not even a star had managed to puncture through its ebony richness. She continued through the forest, wincing slightly as she put pressure on her leg. She had made a rookie error earlier and got it caught underneath a root. She shouldn't be out here really, but the constant bickering and sniping from her siblings had finally got to her and when she saw her chance she had slipped away unnoticed.

She wouldn't go far, just a short distance to get some air and some peace and then head back; well that was the plan! She wasn't afraid to be in the forest on her own, but it did seem to be getting thicker and darker and it was unusually silent.

She stopped and listened, nothing! She stood for a while and was about to turn round and head back when the hairs on the back of her neck went up, the stillness of the night suddenly broken by the distant howling of wolves. She decided she had better move quickly before they picked up her scent, but because the sound was coming from behind, she had no choice but to move forward, pushing deeper into the forest.

After what seemed like ages, she could still hear them behind and was struggling to see the ground in front of her, when suddenly out of nowhere the moon appeared bathing parts of the forest with light. Up ahead she could see the glistening of water and hear it as it gurgled and babbled along. Heading quickly towards it she knew what to do, she might be young, but she was savvy and knew if she waded up stream her scent would be lost. The water was cold, causing her to shiver, but she waded through it and as she did so she noticed looming up in front of her was a ruin, a tall tower surrounded by crumbling walls. The tower came down to the edge of the stream . Its stone base submerged, she could see an opening a few feet up; if she could get through that she was sure she would be safe.

She cursed herself for being so stupid; she was going to be in so much trouble. Steadying herself and despite the pain in her leg she jumped and scrambled up the wall and into the gap.

The moon, as quickly as it had appeared, disappeared into the blackness and once again she was plunged into darkness. Her eyes though had now become accustomed to the night and she could see much more clearly. She surveyed the ruins; the tower she was in had a few steps up and then an exit opening out onto a wall. The rest of the staircase and roof of the tower had long gone and Mother Nature had taken over with ivy and lichen covering much of the grey stone walls.

The wall was wide enough to walk along although it was crumbling away in parts. She could see that at the other end of the wall was a small building offering what looked like some shelter. She made her way steadily along so as not to slip or knock some of the stones off, which would have sent out a signal to the wolves.

She reached the other end where there was a dilapidated building with trees growing through it, and a small alcove which overlooked what once might have been a courtyard. A pile of dry brown leaves had blown into the alcove so she decided to make herself comfortable before deciding what to do next. The wolves had stopped howling and she listened hard for any sounds, but once again the forest was silent and she was as happy as she could be that she had given them the slip. Glad of her warm coat as the night air had started to turn chilly, she snuggled into the leaves as best as she could to give her some more protection. The sound of an owl screeching once again broke the silence and then out of the dark it came in full flight a beautiful white barn owl. It sensed her slight movement and turned, caught her eye and then flew up and over the wall and was gone.

She must have fallen asleep because she woke to the sound of something striking stone; it was loud and echoing through the ruins. She was sure she could feel the ground trembling. The moon was out again and there was a bright glow coming from the old courtyard area below. As quietly as she could she raised her head from its resting position and peered down. She could not believe what she saw; a large magnificent looking stag with antlers the size of small trees was striking the ground with its hoof; she was convinced she could see sparks and yes she wasn't mistaken the ground was definitely vibrating.

However, the most surprising thing of all was the colour of the stag, pure white! She gazed in wonder too scared to move, although she didn't feel afraid, not one bit, she just didn't want to frighten him off. The stag though sensed her presence, because it suddenly lifted its head and with nostrils flared stared her straight in the eyes.

They must have remained like that for at least 10 seconds. She could see the warmth of her breath hitting the cold air making soft white plumes, but noticed there was nothing coming from the stag. Suddenly it gave out one almighty roar which reverberated around the ruins and sent waves of sound across the forest. She stood up, not losing eye contact, unsure what to do next. The stag however, dropped its head in almost a bow and then at almost the same time the moon disappeared and it leapt and literally vanished into thin air. She was rooted to the spot, not quite believing what she had just witnessed. Wait till she told the family, what a tale she had to tell!

She was just debating about making her way down into the courtyard area, when a crashing sound could be heard coming from the trees, followed by a loud call; her father, she would recognise that call anywhere. Then there he was, leaping across the stream with ease. As stags go, he was big, although he wasn't as big as the white stag, but in her eyes he was just as magnificent. In all her excitement of seeing him she leapt from the alcove and down into the courtyard, forgetting about her sprain until her legs buckled beneath her and she cried out with pain.

Within seconds her father was next to her using his nose to encourage her to stand. 'Hurry little one, we must get going, we don't have long before the wolves will be back on our trail.' He didn't sound cross to her, just concerned.

'I'm sorry for leaving home' she stammered, 'but you won't believe what just happened'!

Her father stopped her and looked her in the eyes. 'You can tell us all about it when we are safe, but for now let's go. Can you walk?'

'Yes, I'm ok', she replied and started heading across the stream and into the forest.

Behind, her father had stopped just before the stream; he lifted his head up high and roared; it was an unusual sound and one which she had not heard before. She thought she heard an echo and felt the ground tremble, but she couldn't be sure. Her father was now nudging her along; his call had been a thank you to the great white stag, a mythical creature who helped those lost or afraid in the forest. He was grateful for the guidance it had given him, but hoped he would not need its help again.

Andrea Cook – 2023

Funny Noise

Our sessions often start off with a bit of a chat and catch-up and from them topics often come up. Things that go bump in the night was the inspiration for this one.

I thought I heard a funny noise as I lay in my bed
Shhh, there it was again, or is it in my head?
I try hard not to breathe as I strain to hear
Yes, there it was again, loud and clear
Perhaps a fox was checking out the contents of our bin
If it was, he was making a pretty awful din
But it sounded like it was from indoors
Perhaps it was mice underneath the floors
There would have to be an army of them to make such a sound
And this noise was definitely from above the ground
I will try and ignore it and go back to sleep
No, I will get out of bed and go and take a peek
I hope there is no prowler lurking in the dark
Now I can hear the beat of my heart
Boom, Boom, it goes as it pounds loud and clear
Calm down, calm down, there is nothing to fear
I head down the stairs as quiet as I can
Oh, I wish I had a large frying pan!
The noise now sounds different than it did before
And I pause for a second outside the kitchen door
I throw it open wide and switch on the light
And I am greeted by the most alarming sight
My two cats wreaking havoc and I think I know why
As something small and furry quickly scuttles by
They have brought in a mouse which has escaped their claws
And now it's desperately trying to avoid their jaws
What to do, I just can't decide
I really don't like mice I just want to hide
I know, I'll wake up my husband, he's the man of the house
And he can deal with the mess, the cats and the mouse!
I close the door and creep back upstairs
Give my husband a nudge and say 'I hear funny noises I'm scared'

Andrea Cook – 2023

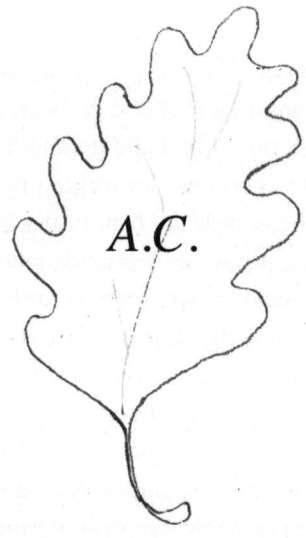

A.C.

Alan Fryer

In my teens I wanted to write sci-fi – but then, so does everyone. Then I was in a local rock band – but this was Liverpool in the 1960s, it was the only way to avoid football. And so I started writing songs. I found the words much easier than the music.

After Uni I became a software developer. The manuals we used were dreadful – you'd spend an hour deciphering a page of techno-gobbledegook, and finally realise it meant "Press Start". So I decided I could do better. I wrote two books about computers, freelance, and they were published. So I then moved from software development into writing the manuals for our products. They were huge tomes – but I made sure I wrote in plain English!

Meanwhile I got interested in Gilbert & Sullivan's comic operas, and then in folk music. Both of these influenced the songs I wrote – mainly, I started to make them funny. But sometimes I just couldn't think up music for words I'd written – so I'd decide they were a poem. And eventually I admitted to myself that often I was, in fact, writing poetry!

Early in 2023 I started volunteering at the Swindon 105.5 Community Radio Station. When the station manager, Shirley Ludford, saw my interest in writing, she suggested I join the writers' group attached to the station. So here I am!

Better In The Dark

There was the night I told my wife
That she looked better in the dark;
Let me explain, for dear life,
Just what I meant by this remark.

I meant – I meant this all along –
I found it more romantic so.
The words just sort of came out wrong.
My gosh, she has a sharp big toe!

"And you a poet, too!" she said;
"At least, you seem to think you are!
Yet you can't work out in your head
The words to say that I'm your star!"

Since then she's fed me sprouts and stuff;
She says it's better for my health.
But I'm not fooled by all that guff;
It's just a punishment by stealth.

And so I bought her roses next;
It didn't help – they made her sneeze.
What could I do, with her so vexed?
At last I went down on my knees;

And said, "My love, you look your best
When I'm so dazzled I can't see!"
Oops – no! I s'pose you've guessed the rest:
It's cold out here without a key!

Alan Fryer - 2024

Cat In A Space Warp

*My daughter had a new extension built. This meant removing the sunroom, which she gave to the next-door neighbours to erect on the back of **their** house. Its external door, with cat-flap, naturally went with it. The cat was subsequently observed sitting outside it, looking most perplexed...*

As family cat, I feel I should be treated with respect;
And things that do my head in count as cruelty and neglect.
My humans caused a huge upset with noisy great machines;
My cat-flap's in a space warp now! I don't know what it means!

Now from the day the world began, that flap led right inside
My warm and cosy sunroom where the world could be defied.
There were my food, my drink, my toys, my basket nicely done;
And little Davy's iPad, nice and warm to sit upon.

I know it's my own cat-flap, as it looks and smells the same,
But in another garden it just doesn't play the game;
For if I go in through it I'm in quite a different world –
No vinyl, but a carpet; and no food, but objects hurled!

And people saying, "Shoo, daft puss, this isn't where you live!"
And stamping with their feet with all the fury they can give.
Besides, the house is back to front, the children are all wrong,
And where my basket ought to be there's just a doggy pong.

It's way beyond my feline brain, it's horribly surreal;
These humans do some crazy things, but how can someone steal
A whole entire universe, and turn it inside out
And upside down; and leave a cat a seething mass of doubt?

S'pose Einstein could explain it, but then Einsteins don't exist
Within the feline species, though we sometimes get the gist
Of what these crazy humans do; but this "one step beyond" –
It turns dimensions upside down, and lets all sense abscond!

But if I peer over at that house that's strangely grown,
I see a human who does look and smell just like my own.
She's banging on a food bowl with a spoon! Ah, that makes sense!
Forget the metaphysics, Puss. Just jump across the fence!

Alan Fryer - 2024

My Daughter Has A Husband

Although I mostly write humorous poems, I did once write an anti-war poem by mistake. Just occasionally a true family story comes along that just begs to be told. In this poem, I simply wrote down exactly what really happened. Then I looked at it, and thought, "Ooh! That's an anti-war poem, that is!" But it is the only anti-war poem I know of that has a happy ending!

My daughter has a husband; she met him while in France;
We went to Flanders, where she worked, to meet and shake his hand;
We met upon the battlefields of that sad and silent land.
We walked around the graveyards we'd all always meant to see;
We called from trench to opposing trench – so short the space between;
And we said how very stupid all our rulers must have been;
Yes! We said how very stupid all our rulers must have been!

My daughter has a husband; we took a summer trip;
We all drove through the Rhineland, and then on into the East;
Past where the Iron Curtain used to cage the iron beast.
We talked of how the missiles used to point across our world;
Of border guards, and nuclear tests, and deadly rays unseen;
And we said how very crazy all our rulers must have been;
Yes! We said how very crazy all our rulers must have been!

My daughter has a husband; we finished off our trip
In Dresden – on the Elbe – that's a place once more alive;
Admired the reconstruction since the raid of forty-five.
A fire-storm like an atom bomb – the war already won!
Was it just vengeance for the Blitz, or done to scare Stalin?
And we said how very ruthless all our rulers must have been;
Yes! We said how very ruthless all our rulers must have been!

My daughter wed her husband in his family's parish church:
The Kreuzkirche in Dresden – the Church of the Holy Cross;
Restored in all its glory as it was before the wars!
So she became Frau Grützner, and so beautiful she looked;
We sang as our two families watched the future crush the past;
And we said how we the people show you can get it right at last;
Yes! We said how we the people show you can get it right at last!

Alan Fryer - 2010

Coronation Cuppa

I wrote this during the few days after the coronation of King Charles III. I do feel a little guilty for having written it, because it complains (very mildly and light-heartedly) about people who were very well intentioned. But it does express appreciation as well!

I went to a live-streaming place,
To crown ol' Charly Three;
Because I am a royalist; and –
We might be offered tea!

I thought there'd be an interval;
That's usually the way;
A huddle round a steaming urn;
But – not on this great day!

Archbishop put a jewelled crown
Upon our monarch's head;
And as my heart swelled up with pride,
A voice behind me said:

"Ah, would you like a cup of tea?
Perhaps a custard cream?"
I shouldn't be ungrateful, but
It made me want to scream!

He went to be anointed then,
Behind a modest screen;
A hush fell on the Abbey, for
So sacred was this scene.

"Did you say coffee? Was it tea?"
It's nice to have a choice.
And yet I could have done without
That interrupting voice.

"Do you like sugar in your tea?"
I want to whisper, "Shush!"
It's nice to be so waited on,
But please – a bit of hush!

And then the live-stream ended, just
Before the Royals came out
To stand upon their balcony.
So that was up the spout!

And so I watched again at home,
Upon my Sky-box thing;
And felt at last I had the chance
To say, "God save the King!"

Alan Fryer - 2023

Finding A Phone

I hear it – underneath the cushion!
I hear it – there, beneath the cat!
I hear it – in a sort of fashion;
I'm sure – or could it be a gnat?

Somewhere in this messy house, I've lost my mobile phone!
They say just ring from somewhere else – you'll hear its dulcet tone.
I'd ring from the old landline, but its cordless handset's lost;
I've got to find my smartphone! I remember what it cost!

And so I ask my daughter, "Will you ring my phone from yours?
I know your credit's getting low – but it's a noble cause!"
"Credit?!" cries the dear child. "My battery's dead flat!
I'll have to plug it in for hours, before I can do that!"

And so I try the neighbour next – I call across the fence,
"Hey Fred – please call me on my phone – it costs but a few pence …"
And so he does – I see his hand a-reaching for his phone;
His fingers tap the glistening screen. I'll soon hear my ringtone!

I hear it – underneath the cushion!
I hear it – sort of faint "brom-brom";
I hear it – in a sort of fashion;
But where could it be coming from?

I hurl the cushions in the air, I overturn the table,
I search the bureau, clear the shelves – as far as I am able.
And now I think I'm getting warm – I search once more, with feeling,
The clothes piled on the bedroom chair – upon the floor I'm kneeling!

I hear it – if this works, don't knock it!
I hear it – I'm as close as that!
I've found it! It was in my pocket...
"Thanks Fred!" But I feel such a prat!

Alan Fryer - 2023

Loo Light

This poem is on a slightly niche subject – the light switch in the outside toilet in the Richard Jefferies Museum. The 19th century writer grew up near Swindon, and his house is now a museum and arts centre. I was at a weekend poetry workshop there, and after some misadventures in the dark I offered feedback on this light switch – well, ok, I grumbled about it. So they challenged me to write a poem on the subject! I stayed up all night writing it, and performed it next morning.

Little light upon the wall;
Could you be a switch at all?
Pipes lead to you – surely you're
The stopcock for the water pure?
If I press you, this place might
Flood with – anything but light!

After I have used the loo
In total darkness, still I do
Need to find the towel and soap;
All right – there's only one faint hope:
Press that green light on the wall!
Nothing happens – nowt at all!

Wait! It has a white surround,
Like the bell on buses found;
Surely that's not what you press?
Try it – no, there's no success.
Did the darkness deepen there?
Or was that only my despair?

But – I pressed just the left side.
Left's the only side I tried!
What if only right is right?
Try it – see if right gives light.
Yes it does – the room goes bright!
This garden loo's a glorious sight!

It's actually a good design;
Once you know, it works just fine!

Though at first your brain it mocks,
It solves that age-old paradox
That's plagued mankind since Noah's Ark:
How find the light switch in the dark?

Little light upon the wall,
Your secret should be known to all!
So I hope this little rhyme
Will enlighten for all time
All who wonder how it's done:
How you switch the loo light on!

Alan Fryer - 2019

Note: I think I read somewhere (but I can't remember where) that in pre-Roman times part of the test to qualify as a druid was to write a poem overnight on a set subject, and recite it in the morning. So maybe I could be a druid now! But I think you had to lie in a bath of cold water all night while composing it. Maybe I don't qualify after all.....

Songs Of Hope And Hatred
(subtitle: The Seeds of Spring)

Another accidental anti-war poem – though this is more of an anti-anti-war-song poem. In May 2021, at a folk club meeting on Zoom, someone remarked that music festivals for peace don't work. This set me thinking back over conflicts since the beginning of the 20th century, asking myself which efforts to turn enmity into peace and friendship actually have worked.

Now grim-faced men and women all stand straight-backed and salute;
The flag flies bravely in the breeze, there's gloss on ev'ry boot;
While down the street another band sing songs of love and peace,
And how if we'd just all be good and kind all war would cease.

Across a line drawn on the map, a wall built on the sands,
The losers search the rubble for toy bears and children's hands;
And hear us sing our songs of peace, our songs of peace and love;
We winners in our safety sing the grace of God above.

Our songs of hope and hatred float across the great divide,
To those whose loss and agony keep us safe in our pride.
It's not the flags that will bring peace, and not the songs we sing;
But helping former foes step forth and sow the seeds of spring.

The anthem swells, the tears spring forth, the guns gleam in the sun;
While songs protest at wicked war. Is this how peace is won?
How piously the right-wing praise the flag that flies above;
How piously the left-wing sing that all you need is love.

How quietly, how quietly the true peacemakers walk,
In corridors and conference rooms, cajole old foes to talk;
And so the lonely diplomat slogs on her weary way,
Builds bridges slowly down the years while we just sing and pray.

On our side of the map's thin line we're good kind peaceful folk;
So we must kill them over there who could bring our death-stroke.
On their side of the map's thin line they're good kind peaceful folk;
So they must kill us over here who could bring their death-stroke.

There's more to peace than just one word; there's more to understand,
To work well with our neighbours and accept each other's hand;
Not booted feet nor songs of peace address the dreadful pain
That makes men mad so that they bring pain on themselves again.

We all want peace – but how, in such a complicated land?
The human dove finds little time for sleeping in the sand;
Takes messages, negotiates for each side's needs and fears;
Thrice blessèd are these peacemakers, whose names one seldom hears.

Our songs of hope and hatred float across the great divide,
To those whose loss and agony keep us safe in our pride.
It's not the flags that will bring peace, and not the songs we sing;
But helping former foes step forth and sow the seeds of spring.

Alan Fryer - 2021

Notes:

- *"Helping former foes step forth ..." refers to the UK and US helping Germany and Japan rebuild after WWII. Well, it worked, didn't it? They've been our good friends ever since.*

- *I said "**her** weary way" because I had Mo Mowlam in mind.*

- *Some lines are quotes from the conversation that followed the remark at the folk club.*

Parsnip Poem

When people find out that you write comic rhyme,
They like to suggest new ideas;
And there was a man that I met at one time,
In a chat o'er a couple of beers,
Suggested a song about parsnips, forsooth,
Though I told him that parsnips aren't funny;
But I've tried really hard, and I've found it's the truth:
I just can't find the fun in a parsnip.

The man that I met who requested this rhyme
He was head of all veg down at Sainsb'ry;
A very nice man, as I thought at the time,
As every head veg'table should be.
This isn't a song – it's a poem, at best.
I'm afraid that is all I could manage!
There are many good themes I could tackle with zest;
But I can't find the fun in a parsnip.

I could write of roast beef, or of food from the sea,
Like in fishy French films that end "Fin" (Fin!)
      [pronounce as English 1st time, French 2nd time]
Or the bangers and mash that I have for me tea;
Or the cabbage I throw in the bin (bang!)
      [mime banging down bin lid]
Potatoes plus peas possess positive panache,
Pomegranates – perfection personified!
Pumpkins produce perfect pie (dice or mash).
But I can't find the fun in a parsnip.

Proposals for poems send post haste to me;
Or I might even welcome a heckle,
I'll ponder your plea over peppermint tea
If someone will boil me a keckle.
You can tell that I'm desperate to finish this rhyme,
Before I begin vegetating!
Ask for love, war or shipwrecks; but I beg you, next time,
Please don't press a poor poet for a parsnip!

Alan Fryer - 2021

Pothole

I heard that a man had decorated a pothole with toys, to draw attention to it. His campaign was good-humoured, and he certainly didn't "crunch" the toys he put down. So this poem is purely fictional and not about him or any other real person. But I acknowledge him as my inspiration.

There was a man who on a whim
Decided potholes were too grim;
And when a pothole burst his tyre
He turned the full force of his ire
Upon the council. Good for him!
He woke them from their slumber dim!

He made a doll up as the mayor,
Another as the town clerk there;
And some more as the whole shebang
Of councillors and all that gang.
And with the pothole full of rain,
A tiny swimming pool they gain!

He took a dolly's deck chair then;
In fact, he took a set of ten.
Umbrella from a cocktail glass;
Dolls' loungers of the highest class;
A fine doll's hammock; better yet,
At last a doll's house patio set.

He placed the council round their pool,
On chairs and hammock, nice and cool.
The sun shone gently on the scene;
A nicer sight there's never been.
But what's that tremor? What faint ghoul
Advances with intention cruel?

No need for voodoo pins and such;
It's just him letting in his clutch;
He's got into his 4 x 4;
Now he's approaching with a roar!
And then the crunch! Go bang the drum!
He's sent the lot to kingdom come!

Alan Fryer - 2024

The Day When My Jenny Comes Back

The first verse should be very fast and jaunty. Then each verse should be slightly slower than the previous one; the last two verses should be very slow and creaky indeed. Then the last line should be a delighted triumphant shout!

I'm saving myself for the day when my Jenny comes back.
When she went off with Danny I really was awf'ly upset.
You can see it won't last; I'll be here when she calls;
So I'm saving myself for the day when my Jenny comes back.

I'm saving myself for the day when my Jenny comes back.
I went to their wedding and Danny was awfully kind.
He's a nice enough bloke, but he's just not her type;
Be all over by Christmas and then she'll be back in my arms.

I'm saving myself for the day when my Jenny comes back.
Two kids, two careers must be an intolerable strain.
Yes the cracks will show soon; she and Dan will soon part;
So I'm saving myself for the day when my Jenny comes back.

I'm saving myself for the day when my Jenny comes back.
With three kids and that great big house, can a marriage survive?
Must be run off her feet! Daniel won't understand;
If she loses her figure he really won't care for her then.

I'm saving myself for the day when my Jenny comes back.
With four kids in college and him in the City all day,
He can't be what she needs – this Sir Daniel of hers!
So I'm saving myself for the day when my Jenny comes back.

I'm saving myself for the day when my Jenny comes back.
This cruise they've gone on with their grand-kids is just showing off.
Just wait, soon she'll be bored; she'll come running to me;
With a second-hand Ford we could take fish and chips down the prom.

I'm saving myself for the day when my Jenny comes back.
Can afternoon tea on the lawn every day be her style?
When the Jenny I knew used to dance until dawn!
So I'm saving myself for the day when my Jenny comes back.

I'm saving myself for the day when my Jenny comes back.
If I scrimp and I save I could get in the same home as them.
But it costs such a lot; could re-mortgage the flat;
And under the same roof each day – who knows what might transpire!

I'm saving myself for the day when my Jenny comes back.
Up in heaven all souls are as close as the angels themselves.
Jesus said so Himself – it's in Matthew 22.
We'll be there for all time … Danny might go to hell!

So I'm saving myself for the day when my Jenny comes back!

Alan Fryer - 2010

The Vegan And The Clothes-Moth

The verses should be recited gently, almost piously. The opening "... clothes-moth(s) ..." of the chorus should be spoken quietly. The chorus should then be declaimed with maximum possible melodrama.

My daughter is a gentle soul, a vegan to the core;
She'd never hurt a living thing; my faith she does restore.
From elephants to honeybees, she wants to save them all;
Respect for ev'ry living soul, however big or small.

Except clothes-moths ... Is that a clothes-moth?
Catch it ! Kill it! Squash it! Squish it! Let death be its fate!
Cat, come catch it! Claw it! Kill! Devour! Exterminate!
May its short life – not short enough! – be blighted by my curse!
Consign it to oblivion, to Hades, Hell, and worse!

At dressmaking she does excel, exquisite is her work;
But open up her wardrobe door – and see her go berserk!
A cotton dress that took her weeks, now full of holes as lace;
A little clothes-moth comes fluttering out, a big grin on its face.

Oh! A clothes-moth ... Is that a clothes-moth?
Catch it ! Kill it! Bash it! Bish it! Flush it down the loo!
Cat, come catch it! Claw it! Kill! Reduce it to a goo!
May its short life – not short enough! – be blasted by my curse!
I wish upon it cataclysm, catastrophe, and worse!

We nightly feed our urban fox – she buys it Winalot;
A camera in our garden shows the wildlife we have got.
A rat lives in our compost bin: "How sweet its little paws!"
But then, it doesn't eat her clothes like those minute outlaws.

Yes ... the clothes-moth ... Is that a clothes-moth?
Catch it ! Kill it! Mash it! Mulch it! Smash it to a pulp!
Cat, come catch it! Claw it! Kill! Ingest it with one gulp!
May its short life – not short enough! – be battered by my curse!
May it meet Armageddon, apocalypse, and worse!

So, vile insect – meet thy doom!
     [on "doom", clap hands as if squashing a flying insect]

Alan Fryer - 2019

Antikew's Curious Old Masters

This was written to be spoken – hence the phonetic spelling.

When I was a child, there was a parade of shops near where we lived, with one shop that stuck out forward of the rest. So it had a side-wall, at right angles to the other shop fronts. On this rather dismal, Dickensian brick side-wall was something that puzzled me for years – in block capitals, in faded white paint, divided over three lines, were written words that I read out as: "Antikew's curious old masters".

I guessed that Antikew must be a horse, since he had masters – though I was puzzled that he had more than one. I was puzzled by the spelling of his name – it ended in "que", which surely could only be pronounced "kew". As a well-educated child, I was puzzled they had left out the apostrophe before the "s" in "Antikew's", and the "u" before the "s" in "curious".

And why did we need to know his masters were old? In fact, why was this written there at all, on the side-wall of that shabby old junk shop? It didn't actually tell us anything about Antikew, or his masters, or what they were curious about.

Maybe I wasn't all that well-educated after all, because I was well into my teens before I finally deciphered it. I learnt that ANTIQUES are things that are old and rare; that CURIOS are things that are of little use but interesting; and that OLD MASTERS are paintings by famous artists. It was just a list of things they bought and sold!

Alan Fryer - 2024

The Village Hall

One week, the subject we set ourselves to write on was "the village hall" – and I realised I had something to say on the subject!

Once upon a time, in a time not so very long ago, in a country not so very far away, there was a village hall. And once a month, on a Saturday, a farmers' market was held there.

It was a very popular farmers' market, and all the people from miles around went there. They bought beef, and sausages, and lardy cakes, and cooking oil, and greetings cards, and oh, every nice thing you can think of. And nice ladies served coffee and tea and cakes.

But there was just one problem – the poor little village hall had only six parking spaces. And the kerb nearby had only six parking spaces too.

But not to worry! Directly across the road was the village pub. Now, it had a great big huge car park. And it had a nice landlord, with roots in the village going back generations, and he was happy for the people going to the farmers' market to park in his car park. And it was good for his business too, because many of them went to the pub for lunch afterwards.

And so they all lived hap – oh – no – no, they didn't – because ... the landlord retired! And the pub was bought by a horrible ogre.

And scarcely had the new landlord – I mean ogre – moved in, than he put up *signs*. Dozens of 'em, one every few yards all around the car park, saying "Customer parking only. Non-customers will be devoured." Well, no, they said "fined" really, but "devoured" is more traditional.

Now this would have been perfectly justifiable in the middle of a town, where the car park might quickly fill up with non-customers, leaving nowhere for the pub's own customers to park. But this was a quiet little village, and even when the pub was crowded there was still space in the car park. And even when the pub was crowded and the farmers' market was busy, there had always still been space in the car park.

So next farmers' market, oh, woe, woe is me! The people came – and they couldn't park – and they went away again! And they went away sad. And come the next month's farmers' market – nobody came! They knew there was nowhere to park. And so the farmers' market withered away. And funnily enough, the pub's business withered away too. Nobody seemed to like a pub run by an ogre.

But then – the ogre couldn't make a living ... can't think why ... and no-one would speak to him – and after six months he gave up and sold the pub! And the man who bought it, the *new* new landlord, do you know what he did? He pulled down all the nasty little signs. And when people asked, "Can we park in your car park?" he said, "Of course! Welcome!" Soon word got round ... and the next month's farmers' market was as busy and bustling as ever it had been. And soon the pub too was busy and bustling again, and the new new landlord became rich, and beloved by everyone in the village. And they all lived happily ever after! (Except the ogre. I don't know what happened to him.)

Moral: a village pub is part of the community. Any incomer who doesn't understand that is *DOOMED*.

Alan Fryer - 2024

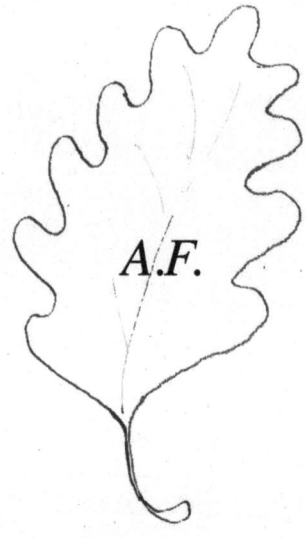

Ross Kitchen

At school I enjoyed two things, reading and chemistry. I disliked English lessons though and writing. Oh how things have changed.

My career was originally in chemistry, working in a laboratory, testing paints and resins. I came to dislike the constant mess and smells though.

Through redundancy, I took the opportunity to switch careers. I changed to working with databases, spreadsheets and reporting to management. It involved lots of writing, something I started to like.

Just before the Pandemic, I started writing. My youngest daughter was unhappy and missing me, as I had moved away for work during an acrimonious divorce.

My Favourite Author

My favourite author Mary (Andre) Norton wrote under the pen name Andre Norton as publishers saw science fiction/fantasy as a male domain at the time.

How did you do it?
So many books
So many worlds
Witch World is one
Women so strong
Jaelithe just one
A favourite of mine
To find a portal
Always on my mind
Fantasy worlds with cats galore
Spaceships and empires
Hive worlds and more
Time travel too
And Multiple worlds
Long before they were cool

Ross Kitchen - 2024

Saint George

The prompt for this one was Saint George.

A new man now
The epitome of England
Sat on his charger
Lance in hand
Dressed in chain-mail
A surcoat of white
Bearing a cross of bright red
So recognisable
Visible from afar
Looking beneath
The original I can see
A soldier for sure
But no chain-mail he
A Roman Legionnaire
Gladius, Pilum and Scutum were his things
Out of Palestine
Of Greek descent
So all the stories claim
A Christian he did declare
That was his true belief
How that would deliver grief
Beheaded at the Emperor's whim
Refusal to recant was a sin
Martyred for his belief
Now a beacon for the weak

Ross Kitchen - 2024

Maypole

Tried to bring a traditional Maypole celebration to life.

A village tradition
For such a long time
The reason long gone
Now just a fun day
Out on the green
Each first of May
A tall Maypole
Set for all to see
Crowned with garlands
And hung with ribbons
Colourful and bright
The crowd arrives
The music starts
Dancers appear
Led by a woman
Queen for a day
The women so grand
Dressed for a ball
Skirts so pretty
Flowers and all
Men in white shirts
Looking their best
They each grab a ribbon
Holding it high
Skipping and bowing
Circling around
Closer and closer
The Maypole is bound

Ross Kitchen - 2024

Country Cottage

Walking down the lane
What a sight greets me
Sat back from the road
Partially hidden in the trees
A country cottage laid bare
It seems to hug the ground
Flint walls that are crooked and bent
Thatched roof that seems to sag down
Now blackened with age
Chimney quite tall, grey smoke and all
A winding path leads to the door
Bordered with flowers
Hedgerows of green
Frame gardens so wide
Hollyhocks and Delphiniums
Stand guard at the rear
Flowers of all colours
Planted at will
Blue, pink, purple and red
So many shades, blend into the next
Butterflies and bees
Contest for the best
Lavender and Honeysuckle scent the air
As l take a deep breath
I could stand here all day
Taking it in
A beautiful English Country Cottage

Ross Kitchen - 2024

Desert

For the prompt Desert, I wanted to show how much life there actually is there.

Hot by day
Light so bright
Cold at night
Stars alight
Moving sand
Dunes so high
Carving rock
Mountains dry
No life they say
But wait and see
Beetles scurry
Lizards dance
Buzzards high
Bones abound
All picked clean
No life around
All underground

No respite here
Just nature raw
Forget your water
A price you'll pay
The winds do sigh
Lifting sand
Blocking sight
Deadening sound
Walking through
Ignoring all
A camera clicks
The picture is his
The essence of desert
Sand everywhere
No life around

Ross Kitchen - 2024

Illustrated by Ross Kitchen

Tropical Paradise

From the prompt: Nature. My first thought was nature red in tooth and claw. Then I came up with this.

A tropical paradise
A fantasy dream
In a riot of green

Such a beautiful place
Such a dangerous place

The water, not such a safe place
Crocodile or piranha
Such a risky place

Snakes in the trees
Big cats too
Watch out for the drop bears
Before they get you
Such a wonderful place

Even the insects join in
Malaria, dengue and so many more
Such an itchy place

Such pretty shades
Warn you of danger
Poisonous or Venomous
You takes your choice
Such a colourful place
Such a beautiful place
Such a dangerous place

Ross Kitchen - 2024

Life

An attempt at a different style of poetry. Each line consists of three words and each word on a line must start with the same letter.

Life, Living, Learning

Existence, Elegant, Ephemeral

Glorious, Green, Growing

Raw, Rife, Reaching

Cawing, Clawing, Cowering

Swiftly, Standing, Striding

Freely, Flying, Forward

Ross Kitchen - 2024

The Master Key

A prompt from my sister Sheryll Martin - Key or Master Key. So I thought of this, after rejecting the idea of someone finding a key, having just written a poem about finding a map.

What a thing to have
A Master Key
For a thief, such a beautiful thing
Working the ships
Careful of slips
Not taking too much on any one trip
Working the levels
Dipping my hand
Never boasting to friends
Careful to trust
Opening rooms
Rifling through stuff
The things I have found
The things I have seen
Selling on shore
Sometimes on-line
Nothing too grand
No diamonds or pearls
Keeping it plain
More for the thrill
A magic card trick
As I sail the high seas

Ross Kitchen - 2024

The Old Baseball Player

The prompt for this was baseball, about which I knew nothing. Spent ages researching baseball terms and then gave up, as an idea about an old player came into my mind.

Stood in the box
Flexing my arms
Swinging my bat
The last of my era
Back from retirement
For one last hooray
The jeers of the crowd
The smile of the pitcher
Stood on the mound
Brings it all back
The sting of a tear
The best in my day
An ace as they say
My card is held up
Comparisons with Ruth
Pitcher now ready
A steely resolve
The ball comes my way
A swing so wild
What can I say
The second no better
The jeers turn to laughs
I loosen my grip
Remember my stance
It all comes back as I ready my bat
Its out of the ground
A home run at last
The jeers have all gone
A few chant my name
I salute with the bat
A last hooray
For a charity day

Illustrated by Ross Kitchen

Ross Kitchen - 2024

The Unhappy Trucker

This started out as an attempt at a villanelle style poem. However I couldn't get the lines to fit. The original idea was to write a poem about an unhappy soldier. My first thought was the word weight. Next however came freight and gate, which flicked my mind to an unhappy trucker instead.

Out on the road, in the cab of my truck
Such a big load of freight, I mustn't be late
Night or Day, in the traffic I am stuck

Always behind, such a hard trend to buck
Wave at the guard as I pass the main gate

Dirt roads are a pain, hope I don't get stuck
A block in the road, I'll just have to wait

Such a beautiful truck, now covered in muck
My life a big mess, just hand it to fate

If I had the chance, this job I would chuck
The ship will have sailed, I will have missed my date

Perhaps my next run will change my damn luck
Maybe drive on, to a new life in the next state

Ross Kitchen - 2024

Ashes

The prompt for this was ashes, which gave me the first line.

As the ashes fell so did his tears.
A few friends and relatives stood nearby
Crying or not as the mood took them.
The hole in the ground, dark and uncaring.
A small sapling was placed there
The soil patted down.
Beech trees were her favourite
A brass plaque signifies the uniqueness of this one.
He could remember their first date so clearly.
A romantic meal for two on valentines day.
Two bottles of wine and a pleasant time
Spent chatting about everything and nothing
Two souls set on on fire.
A walk home and a chaste kiss on the cheek.
An eternity spent staring into her eyes.
A less chaste kiss on the lips.
A promise made to meet again.

Ross Kitchen - 2024

Killing The Dragon

A Saint George's Day prompt, write about a dragon.

The dragon had appeared in the sky that morning
Everyone running to the castle in fear
Animals scattering in fright
As it snatched one while still in flight
Then it was gone, everyone in shock
The Sheriff yelled out, 'Back to work it has fled'.
I called out to my friend 'Lets go get that reward'.
Killing a dragon was a key to success
The hand of a Princess, imprinted in my mind
A rush of men followed us out
None of that all for one nonsense here
Only one could claim the kill
Spreading out in the woods, luck was on my side
In a clearing, I found the dragon and prey
It looked at me, so majestic and free
Suddenly I couldn't do it with glee
I lowered my lance
Then saluted my foe
Charging at once, I raised my lance
Knowing I only had the one chance
Luck again with me as my lance struck true
I dismounted at once so pleased with myself
Then noticed the Kit, so sweet and friendly
Two prizes in one
A Princess and a dragon
What a day for me

Ross Kitchen - 2024

The Gathering

Poem based on a prompt from my sister Sheryll Martin, The Gathering. My first thought was to write about someone playing the game. But that meant reading the rules. So l wrote this instead.

A call went out

To those that could hear

1 in 1000, just to be clear

No letter or card

That could be mislaid

A Geas so strong

It could not be gainsaid

Packing their things

Saying goodbye

Crying and screaming

From those left behind

Making their way

The pull is so strong

No need of a compass

No need of a map

Guided by a string

Only they can feel

Reaching the end

Gathering together

What do they find

A new land to claim

A New life begins

Ross Kitchen - 2024

The Spellsword

This is a Villanelle, a French style poem
Format, 5 x ABA, Last verse is ABAA, based on last word
Line 1 repeats on line, 6, 12 and 18
Line 3 repeats on line 9, 15 and 19

Up on a mountain, he made his last stand
A Paladin in armour, holding his sword
A Spellsword in town, trying to sell his hand

Elf at the bar, map and compass his brand
A dwarf in the corner, eating a gourd
Up on a mountain, he made his last stand

Brothers in arms, they formed a swell band
A barkeep close by, strong ale to be poured
A Spellsword in town, trying to sell his hand

Travelling fast, they covered the land
A dragon up high, guarding a hoard
Up on a mountain, he made his last stand

No fresh goods to be had, trail food so bland
No bridges out here, a river to ford
A Spellsword in town, trying to sell his hand

Piles of gold, is that too much to demand
A dragon in front, oh how it roared
Up on a mountain, he made his last stand
A Spellsword in town, trying to sell his hand

Ross Kitchen - 2024

The Battle

This arose from a scene in one of my fantasy novels. In one scene, the characters discuss a memorable battle. I wanted an epic battle poem to go with it and came up with this.

A day to remember
A day to forget
Five thousand of our town
All of our best
Dressed in their finest
Shiny and proud
Axes and shields
All polished and new
Lined up in the sun
I join in a salute
Make a vow to the gods
The enemy in front
Gleaming in white
Such a frightening sight
Lined up for the fight
Outnumbered to start
We screamed out our hearts
Commanded to fight
We beat our shields in delight
Nothing more to say

Demands can't be met
The signal at last
I was beginning to fret
No finesse or technique
We charge right on in
A simple idea
Kill or be killed
My axe finds an Elf
Cuts him on down
Another in front
Will we hold the day
Flat on my back
The light fading fast
I grip my axe tight
As I breathe my last
Five thousand Dwarves
All died that day
Proud to the last
To die that way

Ross Kitchen - 2024

Illustrated by Ross Kitchen

The Photo I Shouldn't Have Seen

The prompt for this was: The photo I shouldn't have seen. It ended up completely different to how I imagined it at first.

Going through my mother's things
Stopped in my tracks by what I held in my hand
My lips quivering with pain
As I tried to prevent the tears

A thing, so simple to see
A photograph, a name, a date
A woman in bed
Baby at her breast

My name on the back
Written in red
The date matched my birthday
Should be so comforting that

The woman was a stranger
Not my mother at all
The conclusion clear
I was adopted after all

Ross Kitchen - 2024

It Was Handmade

The prompt was: It was handmade. So I wrote about a patchwork quilt, that belonged to my Great Aunt.

It was hand made, a patchwork quilt from another time
Nearly two hundred years old
An incredible age for something so plain
So tatty, yet after all those years still so fine
Some of the squares, embroidered with care
Some seemed as good as new, others frayed beyond repair
The time and effort involved, beyond compare
The stories it could tell, the people it had warmed
So rare and simple, a window into the past
Who now does embroidery or sewing
The backing and stuffing so ripped and torn
Hours spent, cutting and clearing it away
The experts all agreed, take it apart piece by piece, cover each in silk, never to be seen
Such a horrible thing to do, to someone's work of art
Taking plenty of of pics I rolled it in a sheet
Plans to display it on a wall, dashed by life
Perhaps one of my daughters will take my place
My favourite piece almost unnoticeable in one corner
E.S.Trull, 1842, my great, great, great-grandmother

Ross Kitchen - 2024

Mother

A prompt from my sister, Sheryll Martin, so I wrote about mine.

A mother to me
Odd as can be
Favourite for sure
At least among the boys
Still so hard to please
No praise for me
Taught me to read
Always pushing me to learn
Men should be strong
No emotions should show
Treat women with respect
Pressed to wed
As early as can be
Yet no girl l found
Was suitable it seemed
Always in town
But no time for me
Missing her grandchildren
But no change l see
Self centred as could be
But still a mother to me

Ross Kitchen - 2024

Suicide

A poem about my struggles with depression and suicidal thoughts.

Such a final thing to do
Such a personal thing to do
Such a selfish thing to do

I sat in a field
All through school lunch
Wrestling with thoughts too dark to speak
A knife to my wrist

No one to judge
No heaven or hell
No soul to save
No soul to condemn

Just me on the edge
Too scared to go forward
Too scared to go through

A scar on my arm
A memento to show
Of a life in turmoil

Thoughts of death always close by
Life carries on as I turn away
My daughters now lighting my way

Ross Kitchen - 2024

End Of The World

An apocalyptic Story

It was the end of the world
Such a clichéd view
And so untrue
Humanity maybe
But not a world so blue
People shouting about
Such a loud to do
Thousands march out
Nothing they can do
The Politicians all gone
Bunkers and hideaways strong
No more laws any more
What will we do
Hunker down on our own
To wait for the end
Maybe party with friends
Such an infamous end
Now the time ticks along
As the whisky is downed
We all sing a song
Avoiding a frown
Where is the hero
Come to save the day
No one in sight
As the world burns so bright

Ross Kitchen - 2024

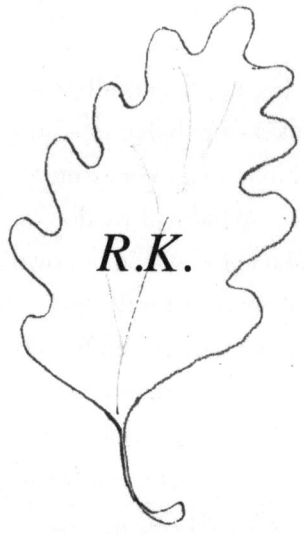

R.K.

Rosemary Lewis

It was late in 2013 and a typical autumnal day when I visited Liden library to update my library ticket. I'd just taken early retirement and decided I needed to dust off my ticket and visit my local library more, in between my yoga and gym lessons. This was for me and not just for the grandchildren!

As I walked up to the entrance there was a large poster by the door. Irene had written it. "Anyone interested in writing turn up here on Friday at 10.30."

Anyone interested? You bet I was! When we had moved to Swindon from South London in the late 80's I'd enrolled at a creative writing group evening class at the then Greendown school and joined a writing group in Haydon Wick. I'd always enjoyed reading and writing and loved sci-fi and historic novels. Then the writing group closed down and work and life got in the way and my writing took a back seat. Seeing the poster just as I retired was meant to be, I decided! Thank you Irene. The rest, as they say, is history.

The Earring

We were given a couple of choices of topic for this particular week: Lost and Found, The Sense of Sight, so I decided to encompass both of them in Essie's Story.

Absent-mindedly rubbing her ear lobes as she watched her mother baking, Essie was suddenly jolted from her daydreaming. Oh no. She had lost one of her earrings. She'd only been gifted them yesterday. Under a full moon shining brightly in the clear sky, Tay had shyly given them to her the previous evening. She was sure that, if she could have seen his young handsome face more clearly in the silver light, she would have seen that his cheeks were flushed. She had been thrilled by the present. Tay was learning his trade with Ull the blacksmith. The metal work on the earrings was intricate and beautiful. Tay had obviously put a lot of care, and dare she hope love, into making them. Her tummy did its usual little somersault as she thought of Tay. But now she had lost one of the earrings and she had hardly worn them! Tears sprung to her eyes. She glanced out of the doorway in the direction of the blacksmith's, a plume of smoke rising up into the clear spring air. Tay would be working hard. She felt her bare ear lobe again. How carelessly stupid of her. She thought back to yesterday evening. Perhaps she had lost her earring in the long grass on the edge of the settlement where she and Tay would go and lie in the warm evenings. She glanced at her mother's back. She was busy by the fire. Essie should have been helping her. They were alone as her father had rushed out earlier to a meeting with the other elders.

"I'm going to fetch some water, mother." Essie grabbed the leather bucket and edged her way out of the hut, picking the rough path to the grassy glade ringed with trees and bushes, her eyes carefully scanning the ground. She prided herself on her sharp eyesight. The sun was shining brightly and she hoped she might see a brown glint of metal in the grass. But to no avail. Perhaps she should have checked her sleeping place back in her parent's hut. The earring could have fallen into the straw. She turned, ready to go back home.

Suddenly she heard shouting and then screaming. She looked in the direction of the settlement. Smoke was rising into the air but it was much more than the previous plume of smoke from the blacksmith's. More panic-filled screams reached her ears as well as deep angry roars and shouting in a language she didn't understand. And then a high-pitched shriek rose above all the other noise. The hairs stood up on the back of her neck. Instinctively she turned back towards the woods and ran and ran…………

*****

Seth looked at the scan image of the settlement on the screen. The outline of a grave could easily be seen on the edge of the screen some distance away from the site of the village they had been excavating. The bypass would miss it but the slip road would not. The young man could feel his excitement rising. They needed another scan focussing on that outer area. There might be other graves nearby.

He walked over to where a digger was already carefully scraping the top layer of soil away. As it went deeper Seth anticipated seeing the layer of charcoal that they had seen when they had excavated the nearby settlement. But there was no layer here. No signs of the catastrophic fire which must have devastated the nearby dwellings. But there was a glimpse of bones.

He lowered himself into the newly dug ditch and carefully scraped and brushed the earth away from the bones. Eventually the shape of a skeleton emerged, hunched over in a foetal position. He cast a professional eye over the bones. He thought it was probably a woman. Unlike the bones found in the nearby settlement there was no obvious signs of trauma. And it looked as if she had been laid out with care. A filigree, possibly copper, necklace still hung around the neck vertebrae. Remnants of a pottery beaker lay at her feet. As he brushed carefully round the skeleton something small caught his eye. He chuckled. The thought that he always prided himself on his sharp eyesight popped into his mind. This could have been so easily missed. Something glinted in the soil below the skull. He carefully picked it up and gently brushed away the earth. A small earring, probably copper as well, as it held a greenish tinge; the craftsmanship was beautiful with exquisite metal tracery. It might well have been made by the same hand as the necklace, although perhaps an earlier piece as it looked less expertly made. Nevertheless, it was lovely. He bagged the earring up and, when the skeleton had been gently lifted away, he examined the earth around where the skull had been to try and find the other earring. He then dug further in the ditch but to no avail.

He looked up from the ditch at the skeleton again. Bones in the nearby settlement had been broken and hacked and most were badly charred. A raid by another tribe maybe? But this find was different. The bones showed signs of wear and tear and the spine was twisted but showed no signs of abuse. He turned to climb out of the ditch and his eye was caught again by something jutting slightly out of the trench wall. Was that another bone? It was getting difficult to see. A voice interrupted his thoughts.

"How are you doing, Seth? The light is fading. Time to call it a day."

He looked up. The lead of the dig, Cate, was standing over him. She grinned at him.

"Good work on the skeleton. An older woman by the looks of things? And you found some jewellery? And a beaker there as well. She may have been of high status then."

Seth smiled back.

"Yes, really pleased. I've only found one earring though. Perhaps a custom we are unaware of? "

"Oh ok. Let's have a look at it"

Cate gasped. "Oh, it's exquisite". She looked more closely at the earring, a puzzled look on her face.

"Have you only just found this earring? It looks very familiar. "

"Just this morning," Seth replied. "I hadn't shown it to anyone. I was trying to find the other one. But no luck so far."

Cate frowned. "It's beautiful. And so unusual." Suddenly she gasped and her face lit up in excitement.

"Come with me to the finds tent and bring that with you."

They got to the tent and she reached for a plastic box containing finds from the nearby settlement. She looked carefully through the artefacts of scorched crockery shards and metal work.

"Here it is."

Triumphantly she held up an almost identical earring.

"We found it in an area that was probably a wooden hut. Larger than the others. Possibly belonged to someone of high rank. The same scenario as the other dwellings though. A thick layer of charcoal in the earth layers. Possibly burnt straw? And this was found in that layer."

Seth smiled. Was the hut where the young woman had lived? Had she tried to run away? And did she lose her earring in the panic? Had she survived the massacre? The signs were that she had. And who had made her beautiful jewellery? She had probably lost almost everything along with her earring but now it, and she, had been found.

*****

Essie looked on in contentment as her grandchildren played in the clearing near to where she sat. She closed her eyes and raised her face to the bright sunlight. The warm weather was good for her bones and she felt more relaxed. The settlement they had started when Tay had found her, and they had travelled some distance away from the massacre, was more secure than the old one and the view from their hut on the top of their hill was breathtaking as well as practical. Any unwelcome visitors could be easily seen in the distance.

Essie opened her eyes and looked toward the plume of smoke on the edge of their settlement. Their son was the blacksmith now. Tay's arm had troubled him more as he got older. A reminder, apart from the scar down his face, of that awful day. She sighed. She fingered the beautiful necklace Tay had made for her after the birth of their first child. He had wanted to make her another earring to replace the one she had lost but she refused. The gods would find it for her in their own time. She shifted. She was getting tired. Soon, she knew, she would see the gods for herself. She had asked Tay to bury her back by the old settlement where their lives had begun. And where Tay had given her those earrings as a token of his love which had endured for years. And when the gods decreed Tay would join her. She raised her face once more as the sun rays touched her old skin. She was content. The gods would take care of her.

Rosemary Lewis - 2024

Illustrated by Dona Allen

The Stone

We were given the title 'The Stone' to write about..

She squeezed her young grandson's hand tightly. He had been looking eagerly through her old books and had suddenly declared he wanted to go on a bug hunt. She looked around her. Where would she go? Would she take him there? She couldn't think of anywhere better but sadly she secretly didn't think they would be successful. She looked at his upturned young face, flushed with excitement. He had a tatty looking rucksack containing a magnifying glass and The Book, slung over his shoulders.

"I think it's time I showed you the Stone. You are old enough now. We will go there first."

"The Stone, Granny?"

She nodded as they headed off. On their way they laced their way through some strange looking things of varying heights that stood proud in the stark landscape. Some were only waist high. He thought he might have seen them in Granny's old books. She glanced at him.

"Be careful. Don't break anything. They are too precious."

They came to a stop by a large round stone. He looked at it curiously. It wasn't like the stones that were scattered everywhere you looked, old pieces of jagged masonry seared into the ground.

The young boy ran his hand over the stone. It was very smooth and, he thought, very beautiful.

His grandmother prised up the stone with her fingers. She had done this so many times now it was easy to move. What appeared to be a metal disc, with a crisscross etched into it, lay underneath.

"X marks the spot," she murmured. "Treasure Island." She laughed at his puzzled face. "X marked the spot where the treasure was. You know. You've read Granny's old books."

Her grandson had read the precious old books hidden under the floorboards in his Granny's old shack. Granny said his father used to read them when he was a boy but, since the boy's mother had died of the sickness, his father refused to read anything.

With shining eyes, the young boy looked up at his grandmother. "And what treasures did you find here, Granny?"

He knew the answer of course. He had heard the story so many times but he still loved to hear it. She sighed.

"I wasn't much older than you when I found the stone. It was so different from anything else I'd seen. It wasn't blackened or broken. So beautiful I wanted to take it home."

She closed her eyes.

"I had to dig it out with my bare hands. They still say you shouldn't do that without checking the Geiger reading first but I'm still here aren't I? And underneath the stone was this metal cylinder. You could only see the top, like this, at first. But when I eventually pulled it out and found out how to unscrew the lid....... Well then I found the old manuscripts and books with pictures of a world that seemed so wonderful and ...... well green."

"Like the book in my rucksack? The one with the bug on the front?"

She sighed. "Yes. The Ladybird book. Full of pictures and facts about things called insects or bugs. Beetles, butterflies, bees."

The young boy's eyes widened. "There were other pictures, Granny. Plants. And some great big......." He hesitated and she nodded.

"Trees," she corrected. "That's what we walked through. Young trees."

She shut her eyes. She could visualise the collections of metal tins she had found underneath the cylinder of books. Tins of all shapes and sizes but all carefully sealed and labelled with yellowing, faded labels. Maram grass seeds, bracken spores, primrose seeds. A myriad of names that she had heard of but never seen. And then more exciting larger, labelled tins, some with brackets after the names. Hazel nuts, Beech masts, Acorns (Oak), Sycamore wings, Conkers (Horse chestnut), pine cones (Scotch Pine). The tins had rattled excitedly. "Open me, open me," they seemed to cry. "You will have to wait while we grow but generations to come will see us."

And so, she had sown them. She had no idea if they would grow in the seemingly barren, polluted ground but ....

She was jerked out of her reverie by a shrill little voice. "Granny, Granny. Look." He pointed excitedly. "What's that?"

They were standing by a small tree that had delicate yellow tassels hanging from its branches.

"The book says that's a hazel tree," she replied. "And those are catkins. Insects used to come and harvest the pollen but, as there are no insects now, I have to pollinate by hand."

She was sad that she had to do that but proud of the knowledge she had accumulated from reading the books.

"No Granny. Not those. THAT!" He pointed to a catkin, on which hovered a tiny, furry, striped creature, its wings fluttering madly, its legs encased in little yellow bundles.

He took out the old book.

"It's a bee Granny, it's a bee! My first bug!"

Rosemary Lewis - 2017

A Christmas Gift

A few years ago we were asked to write a Christmas-themed poem or story for recording for Radio Swindon 105.5. I'd overheard conversation in a shop about the latest toys that Xmas, so this is it. I based it on no one in particular.

Eileen had debated whether to let her daughter know. Offer to treat her to some new clothes. She couldn't normally afford to do that but now suddenly she could.

She hesitated. That would be behaving like her ex, buying his daughter off with expensive gifts.

Eileen hadn't seen her daughter or grandson for ages. She had eventually managed to talk to her daughter about Christmas last weekend.

"Sorry Mum but Dad is coming to ours this year as we went to his place last year."

But it's not HIS place, she had thought bitterly to herself. It's THEIR place and he wouldn't have been on his own as she had been last Christmas and, by the sounds of things, would be again this year. Curtly cutting the call off, she decided there and then that she would spend the raffle prize on herself. She fingered the Gift Voucher. Yes, a Christmas present to herself. She had spotted a lovely warm coat with faux fur trim in the department store a few weeks ago. Way out of her price range at the time but not now. She hugged herself with excitement. She had never won anything before.

Battling her way into the store crowded with Christmas shoppers, she didn't notice the young mum and little boy until she heard his wail. She turned her gaze to the now sobbing youngster being cuddled by his mum. The young woman was about the same age as Eileen's daughter but there the resemblance ended. Her thin face was pinched and drawn and Eileen could see she was struggling to smile as her eyes welled with tears.

"Robbie, you know that Father Christmas may not be able to bring you that this year. He does know that you have been a very good boy but he has lots of other children to go to as well. Now, let's go and choose a little present for you to give Daddy when you see him tomorrow as you won't see him at Christmas this year."

She felt Eileen watching her and straightened up.

"Daddy hasn't been such a good boy this year." She muttered to Eileen with a grimace. She suddenly looked appalled.

"I'm so sorry. I shouldn't have said that, especially in front of Robbie. But it's been such a hard few months. I'm dreading Christmas Day. Robbie saw one of those robotic dogs in the window. His daddy has a real dog now at his new home and that's what Robbie wants us to have. We can't afford one and anyway it's not practical with me out at work all day. He knows that. And then he saw the robot one.

The child heard her and his sobs started again. He brushed his eyes angrily with his mittened hand. "Sorry, Mummy. Let's go and get socks for Daddy."

His mother bent down and gave him a big hug. "Oh I love you so much. That's all that matters."

She stood up and turned apologetically to Eileen.

"I'm so sorry to bend your ear. We must go. Have a good Christmas."

Hand in hand mother and son started to walk away. Eileen stood there, the voucher burning a hole in her pocket.

"Stop, stop!" She ran after them and caught the young woman's arm.

"This sounds totally mad and I have never done this before – but would you consider spending Christmas Day with me?"

The woman looked startled.

"Apart from my little dog, I'm going to be on my own too. Why don't you get your socks and then meet me in the café for coffee and we can talk about it?

"And," she turned to Robbie with a wink after a quick glance at the robotic dog, "Father Christmas knows where Smudge and I live!"

Rosemary Lewis - 2018

The Fog Walker

It was my turn to think of a theme. I asked three people to pull a word or phrase out of our magic pot: Blizzard, Fog, Dog Walker. Having been responsible for the theme and not having written anything, I wrote this quickly on the Friday morning before our meeting. A bit of nonsense but perhaps it could be expanded into a children's picture book?!

"Hellooooo …" The thin pale figure emerged from the mist. "I'm The Fog Walker." He whispered for dramatic effect.

"Ooooh. A dog walker!" said Myrtle excitedly. She looked around. "Where's your dog?"

The figure looked annoyed and his next whisper was much louder. In fact it was hardly a whisper at all. "Not a DOG walker. A FOG walker!! I walk around and when the weather is misty, or better still foggy like today, then I suddenly appear." He chuckled a wheezy laugh. "And I make people jump. I like that." His white face looked as if it would crack into a thousand pieces as he laughed, but the laugh stopped suddenly and tumbled into the fog. "But you didn't jump. Why didn't you jump?"

The old lady looked at him and grinned. "My goodness me, young man. I'm 92 and I walk with a stick. I can't jump any more. And anyway I might land on your dog. I wouldn't want to do that."

Suddenly it was the tall thin stranger who was jumping. With frustration. "I'm not young, I'm very, very old and I don't have a dog. Are you deaf?"

"Oh, your dog is dead? I'm so sorry. Did someone else jump on him?"

The grey-haired stranger shook his long, thin head. "You're meant to be scared of me," he wailed. "I appear out of nowhere and you're meant to be terrified."

"Oh, I'm not scared of dogs," said the old lady. "I've had quite a few dogs over the years. Used to take them out in all weathers. Rain. I used to like the rain and mud." The old woman looked wistful. "In my wellies."

She smiled at him. "You could be a bog walker if you've lost your dog. Put your wellies on and you'd be fine." His face started to crumple. "You could borrow mine." (In her mind she pictured him in her frog wellies.) Mmm, perhaps they would be a bit of a squash.

His grey face brightened a bit. "I like the rain." But his face changed and he scowled as he repeated slowly. "But, I don't have a dog." He looked at her and sighed. "I'm meant to scare you and I can't at all."

The old woman grinned a toothless grin. "I'm 93, young man. Nothing much scares me. I still walk in all weathers. Snow…"

He interrupted her. "I like snow." His grey face brightened. "I could be a blizzard walker."

The woman stopped in her tracks. "Oh no!" she shivered. "I don't like lizards. Or snakes. I don't like them at all. They give me the creeps. Oh dear. You are scaring me now if you walk lizards. Where are they?"

The grey man was delighted and, with a big smile on his rapidly disappearing face, he dissolved into the fog. A happy ghost. The old woman smiled and went on her way.

Rosemary Lewis - 2024

Illustrated by Julia V H Fryer

My Favourite Toy

We were given the topic: My Favourite Toy. I don't often write poems, but this topic was set during lockdown when we were having weekly video calls. Poems were quicker and easier to transmit and easier to repeat if the connection broke down! Our video calls kept us all sane. Or nearly!

My favourite toy is my first teddy bear.

In fact, he is still in the loft somewhere.

Now totally encased in a clear plastic bag

His growl has long died, his scarf is a rag.

His fur has gone. He is in quite a state

But I can't bring myself to decide his fate.

He is leaking sawdust from everywhere.

Way past repairing my poor tired old bear.

He was my godmother's. She gave him to me when I was a baby.

He's a hundred and three!

He was bigger than me then but as I got older

I would heave him around like a sack on my shoulder.

He would sit in my toy pram and survey all the scene

As I played mum and baby and fed him ice cream.

As I got older, he would sit proud and tall

Amid all my posters of John, George, Ringo and Paul

He's had loads of scrubs over all that time

But now he is past that. His coat is too fine.

Over time, as with us all, he started to sag

He was losing his stuffing. Things were beginning to flag.

He started to leak sawdust. It was all on the carpet.

Needle and thread useless. He was obviously past it.

But he so deserves more than be thrown in the bin.

To say goodbye now would be a mortal sin.

His eyes can still fix you with a pale beady stare.

He may be decrepit but he's my teddy bear.

Rosemary Lewis - 2020

Hot and Steamy

The words that were pulled from Irene's magic tin and that we were given to work with this particular week in 2023 were: Rolled, Unbuttoned, and Wanted.

It was very hot. And very steamy. And that wasn't just due to the weather!

She looked across as he appeared from behind the blue drapes. Sleeves rolled up. Shirt unbuttoned just enough to show a peep of manly chest. The flat stomach suggested an impressive six pack. She looked up. He had the most amazingly sexy chocolate brown eyes. He came up to her smiling sweetly.

"Ah! On the bed and all ready for me," he murmured as he leant over her. He gently took her hand. "There's no need to be nervous."

She sighed dreamily. She wasn't nervous at all. He reminded her of Omar Sharif in Doctor Zhivago. And she was his Lara. She groaned. She had never wanted someone so much. Her body yearned to be ravished. She started to reach her arms up to him to take him down onto the bed with her.

A worried look flashed across his handsome face. His obvious concern for her was moving. He took hold of her arms with strength and purpose. She gasped with desire. He looked back at her with what she hoped was tenderness although she wasn't quite sure.

He spoke urgently to someone behind her.

"The ketamine has obviously kicked in, Nurse. She will pull out her drip in a minute. We need to get started now!"

He looked down at her again.

"It really won't take long to click your knee back into place, Mrs Robinson. Your grandson is here so I'll get him to come and hold your hand while we manoeuvre the joint. Just a quick click. You won't feel a thing!"

"OWWWWWWW!!"

Rosemary Lewis - 2023

Abandoned

Out of Irene's magic tin appeared this combination of words: Old injury, Being Abandoned, Hidden Camera.

Elise's hand shook as she tentatively reached down to the inert bundle hastily wrapped in a dirty blanket. She had spotted it abandoned in a corner of the supermarket car park, wedged between the charity recycling bins. A note was pushed into the folds of the blanket.

"Please look after him." the wobbly handwriting said. "I'm not allowed to keep him." The writing was smudged at the end of the line as if water, or a tear, had fallen on to the paper.

Elise took a deep breath as she carefully peeled back the grubby folds of the blue blanket. She gasped as she saw an arm emerge. It showed signs of an old injury. She pulled the blanket back further. The only sound was her own ragged breathing.

"Oh no." she gasped as she grabbed the limp little figure and pulled it to her chest. "You poor thing. You poor, poor thing."

*****

"Here Bert. Look at this. This looks a bit funny."

The uniformed man pointed to the screen for camera number 2 in car park A. The recycling bins showed up hazily in the black and white image. Someone was huddled next to the bins. Holding something.

"These cheap hidden cameras are rubbish. I can't see properly. What is she doing? What is she clutching?" The security guard pointed to the screen.

"Is she on her own?" Bert peered at the screen, his eyes narrowed to get a better look.

Suddenly a woman appeared, running towards the huddled figure who was straightening up. Her mouth was moving but of course they could hear nothing, reduced to watching the silent scenario.

*****

"Oh Mum, look." Elise held out the bundle to her mother. "He's been abandoned. And he is soaking wet. Can I bring him home? I can't leave him here on his own."

The mother laughed with relief. "Oh Elise, you scared me. I wondered what you had found. You really are getting a bit old for teddies. Haven't you got enough at home already?"

The mother sighed as she looked fondly down at her little daughter.

"Ok. You will have to give him a good wash though and sew up his arm. Come along now before we all get wet."

Rosemary Lewis - 2024

A Cup of Tea

This was another Covid-time poem written for one of our video meetings. The subject was, believe it or not, 'a cup of tea!' I'd like to think things have improved on the streets but sadly they haven't.

What's that? A cup of tea?
No thanks. Not for me.
Got anything stronger?
Keeps me going longer.
What?? Is that a cup of coffee?
Not what I had in mind really!
A sandwich thrown in as well?
Actually, you know I can smell
A bacon bap. Mmm. That would be just right.
I haven't had one since that night
My Stepdad shoved me out in the cold.
I was on my own at 16 years old.
Nowhere to go. No job. No home.
18 years old and I'm still on my own.
Hold on. You want me to come with you?
Eh? Why? What yer gonna do?
No one does somethin' for nothin'. I know.
How can I trust you? Where do I go?
You'll get me a room? I can have one for free?
What do you want? No one does that for me.
You've gotta excuse me for being so wary.
I've had 'offers' before. Some people are scary.
The things they say can make me feel really queasy.
But you seem different. You don't make me uneasy.
What?? No! I ain't joining no army.
I may look a sucker but I ain't barmy.
Oh, that's just what you're called? You help people like me?
That's great. Perhaps I will have that cup of tea.

Rosemary Lewis 2021

The Kiss

I'm fed up with being pestered.
I'm fed up with being pressed.
Yes, I HAVE tried talking to her
She shows no interest.
She doesn't even speak to me
She won't look me in the eye
She's definitely not interested
It's time to say goodbye.
She is really so boring
I don't like the way she's dressed
So please don't keep on nagging
Your voice rings in my head.
No I'm NOT going to do it
I don't care what you say
No, don't bring her to me
I won't do it, no way.
I've tried to get her attention
I DID hear what you said
But I really have had enough
I want to go to bed.
Hold on, what's that in your hand
You say she's bought it for me?
How does she know I like dinosaurs?
She's only a tiny baby.
I don't know why she's suddenly here
I certainly didn't ask her.
Oh go on then, if I really MUST
I'll kiss my baby sister.

Rosemary Lewis - 2018

Note: This is dedicated to my grandchildren.

We're Stuffed

Another seasonal offering. This time from 2018

"I'm not quite sure how it's happened Commander but I think our cover has been blown." He gave a delicate cough. "I think we're stuffed, as they say."

"How do you deduce that, Officer?" The Commander fixed him with a beady eyed stare.

"The populace appears to be preparing for a siege, sir. They are amassing provisions of all kinds. Far more than has been observed on previous reconnaissance missions."

"What type of goods, Officer?"

"Clothing, electrical appliances, cloth objects shaped into images of local fauna, evil smelling liquids in glass bottles, coloured blocks made from animal fat..."

The Commander looked keenly. "Crude bomb making equipment?"

"I don't know, Sir. They certainly don't want them to be found. They are wrapping the objects in coloured paper to disguise the shape and then secreting them in cupboards."

The commander looked puzzled.

"Why are they making cloth fauna? Decoys? What fauna?"

"All sorts sir. Bears. Bunnies..."

"Bunnies? Bunnies?" The Commander's eyes flashed dangerously and his neck wobbled ominously. "You mean rabbits, Officer. Rabbits. You really need to concentrate more on your language modules. And anyway, what possible use are fake rabbits? Why would they hoard those?"

The young officer sighed deeply through his nostril holes and thought hard. "Some sort of ritual? To remind them of their old world before we get to them?"

He gurgled nervously in his throat. "I don't know the significance Sir but there was also a group observed, rather jovial in the circumstances, wearing headgear. They would offer poor protection if that is their function but they may be a camouflage ploy. And some covered their nasal orifices with red bulbs. They look like er... can't think of the name ...er...wet stuff...er... deer?" He grappled for the words. He really should have attached his translation pack this morning.

"What the hell are you talking about? Out with it!"

The Commander looked sternly down his beak at the nervous young officer who was starting to gobble, the wattle on his neck flushing furiously.

"Those…those big animals from the North of the planet. Savage looking head equipment. And that old man with the disgusting white facial hair and red coat uses them to pull his transport. I remember now. Reindeer."

He paused and swivelled his eye nervously towards the Commander.

"The populace are stockpiling a lot of food as well. Months' worth of provisions. Their cooling storages are vastly overloaded. The thing is Sir," the young officer looked uneasy, "The provisions include some unusually large dead birds. My sources tell me they do unspeakable things to the bodies like stuffing them with offal and exposing the carcasses to high temperatures and," he shuddered "they will eat them Sir. Evidently each bird will last for days. Good source of protein in a siege situation."

"The ape men eat flesh, Officer. We already know that."

"Yes Sir but…" his wattle flashed frantically again, "I took the liberty of scanning an image of a carcass on to our Imperial Knowledge Site to see what these birds, called turkeys, look like pre slaughter."

He showed his Commander the screen. The Commander's red and blue mottled face grew luridly scarlet and his short wings flapped in consternation. "But they can't eat those!!" he squawked hysterically. "This is totally unacceptable. They are deliberately inciting us to outright war!"

The young officer swallowed nervously as they stared at their mirror image on the screen in front of them.

The Commander quickly waddled away on his scaly clawed feet to gobble desperately down the space ship's tannoy.

"Invasion to be activated. Invasion to be activated. Flight wings on!"

An hour later, the citizens of Planet Earth looked up towards the heavens to see what was hurtling towards the ground.

"Blimey!" said one, looking at the thick cloud of turkeys hurtling to the ground. "All our Christmases have come at once!"

Rosemary Lewis - 2018

Gales And Trees And Other Things

Irene chose the theme: G&T. This was my interpretation two years ago. Sadly even more relevant now.

"Why," rumbled the mighty oak, "do you pick on me?
I'm only a very old, rather stout, tree.
You're scattering my acorns all around.
Look at them strewn all over the ground.
My branches are heavy with wavy edged leaves.
We trees don't like gales, just a nice gentle breeze."

"Ha. I like to cause mischief," laughed the gale to the tree.
"It's only late summer. Bet you didn't expect me!
I'll blow down your branches, heavily laden with green.
Then you'll block roads, crush cars. Chaos to be seen.
That will teach mankind with its global warming.
There'll be more heat, floods, gales. Let that be a warning!"

Rosemary Lewis - 2022

The Doctor Calls

Occasionally we have a 15-minute challenge. One or two words are picked from our magic tin and we are given 15 minutes to write something. Quite hard to do in the time. The words were: Doctor and Thoughtful.

The doctor looked thoughtful as he picked up the phone.

"Hello, is that Mrs Smith? It's Dr. White here. I believe you have a phone appointment with me? What is the problem?"

"It's this 'ere, Doctor. I don't know what to do about it."

"Erm, Mrs Smith. What precisely is IT?"

"Well, it's just there, Doctor."

"Mrs Smith. This isn't a video call. Perhaps you could be more specific ?"

"Well, its spreading all over, Doctor. And its….." the phone crackles .."quite angry."

"Is it a rash, Mrs Smith?"

"I think so. I can't see it very well."

"Where is the rash?"

"Definitely on the tummy. And then it spreads up. I think. I can't see very well."

"Is the rash raised at all? If you hold a glass to it does it disappear? You said it looks quite angry. Is it red?"

"No, the rash isn't angry, Doctor. It's Fred that's angry."

Dr White hesitates. "Erm, Mrs Smith. Is Fred your husband? Is he angry because you're unwell? That's not very kind."

"Ha ha. Bless you Doctor. Fred's not my husband. He's my goldfish. He's got white spots on him and he is swimming round in circles."

"I know how he feels," mutters Dr. White.

"Pardon doctor?"

"Oh nothing, Mrs Smith."

"Oh look. He has come to the top and he's swimming on his back! Oh Fred! Oh dear. You were too late phoning back, Dr White. I think I'll have to change my doctor. What? I couldn't quite hear you, Dr White. Was that a prayer for Fred?"

Rosemary Lewis - 2024

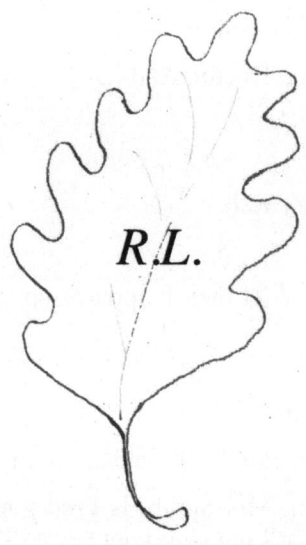

R.L.

Lindy O'Leary

Hello, I am Lindy. I did my first poem at school when I was 10. I love all kinds of poetry especially old ones about the countryside. I find most of my inspiration in the countryside while walking my dogs. I have also dabbled in a few stories since joining the writing group as they really encourage you to dig deep.

I hope you enjoy my work.

The First Daffodil

What beauty does the first daffodil bring,
For winter is gone, and here comes spring,
Though the rain might fall and winds still blow,
We know in our hearts, we have not long to go.

Look all around, look up and look down,
The nights getting lighter, plants on the ground.
The little tight buds, that adorned all the trees,
Are now all starting to open with ease.

The birds singing louder, their joy can be seen,
For everything brown is now turning to green.
So don't you lose faith, just a little more time,
And out of the dullness, the beauty will shine.

Lindy O'Leary

Here's A Nice Place

Here's a nice place,
Let's stop here.
Go to the car,
And get the gear.
Chuck us a sandwich,
And a boiled egg.
Oh there's a fly in my bread.
Got any crisps? That's a nice cake.
A chocky biscuit,
Oh what a nice lake.
Time to go home now
That can't be our mess
If we leave now, no one will guess.

One Year Later

Oh look at that place, it used to be nice
But now full of rubbish
Vermin and mice.

Lindy O'Leary

Corner Field, Day House Lane, Coate

I passed a field of buttercups
They were a pretty sight.
Thought! Make the most of those my dear,
They won't be there tonight.

The machines, they keep on coming,
And soon they won't be found,
Instead of pretty buttercups
There'll be concrete on the ground.

The concrete it soon came
The houses on it too
The natural beauty stripped away
Another human zoo.

So when you see a buttercup
Make sure you give it care.
Or the human machines will come along
And then it won't be there.

Lindy O'Leary

Illustrated by Dona Allen

The Caesarean

I thought that I was dying
An Angel she flew by.
The clouds were of a different colour
And also was the sky.

I wasn't quite sure where I was,
There were noises all around
I heard myself scream out loud,
And then there was this sound.

The angel she came nearer
I felt myself drawn high.
She held her hands out to me,
I thought, please don't let me die.

And then I felt myself float down
Again I heard that sound.
My body it felt different
I tried to look around.

The angel turned into a nurse,
She said to me what joy.
It was really touch or go then,
As she handed me my boy.

Lindy O'Leary

The Helpful Policeman

When walking home one day I saw,
A man in great distress
I said. "You all right mate?" Obviously not,
He said "No it's such a mess
I have locked my keys in my car
I fear I will be late.
An interview I have to go
I know I'll miss the date."
A policeman I was, so you see
I knew a couple of tricks
"Wait there" I says, "I'll help you sir"
Just takes a couple of ticks.
With my gadget, I soon had him in,
He was a grateful guy
He sped off with a wave and grin
And then I heard a cry.
A very well-dressed gentleman
Came running up to me,
"That man just took my car" he said,
"And you just helped him flee."

Lindy O'Leary

Happiness

Happiness, now there's a thing
The cherubs dance, the angels sing.
But does it last for very long
Or die a death, like in a song?
It's what you make it, I have found
You only have to look around.
You never know where it may be
It's out there for us all to see,
The sun comes out it lifts my mind
The breeze it blows my cares behind.
So don't despair if you feel low
Put on your coat and just go.

Lindy O'Leary

Illustrated by Dona Allen

Swindon Town

Swindon town, makes some frown

But, do they actually look around?

There are parks and spaces

To put smiles on faces.

Literature and dance,

To give you a chance.

There is much to be found

Take your nose off the ground.

The people they care

Their community they share

So come and see what is here

Try one of our pubs and have

A beer,

Cheers

Lindy O'Leary

Two Pink Cushions

Two pink cushions,

My dream come true.

Two pink cushions,

I love you.

Two pink cushions,

I knew you cared.

Two pink cushions,

For us to share.

Two pink cushions,

How sweet you are.

Two pink cushions,

We'll go far.

You're coming closer,

I close my eyes.

I feel your breath,

My heart's beat rise.

One pink cushion,

Held to my face.

I cannot breathe,

I leave this place.

Lindy O'Leary

Terrorism

Feeling good, I step off the plane,
Not knowing things won't be the same.
A car is waiting out they came,
I know they're bad I try to run.
Too late, I'm chucked upon the ground,
The guy says "You! Don't make a sound."
"But I'm here to help!! Your people starve."
He says "Who cares, don't make me laugh.
Do you have money? Are you rich?
What's yours is mine, you are my bitch."
"I come in peace, what have I done?"
"This ain't your war," he points the gun.
Months later, no money sent,
I'm roughly handled out the tent.
Kneel down you scum, your life no worth.
Time for you to return to earth,
The gun again held to my head,
He cocks the pistol, I fall dead.

Lindy O'Leary

Dirty Old Town

The rain it pours, he looks outside,
The café's closing, nowhere to hide.
He pushes up from the table,
His head is hurting, he feels unstable.
He goes outside, the thunderclaps,
Heavy rucksack on his back.
Too late to put the tent up now,
The rain it trickles down his brow.
This grey old town, this murky place,
He looks around, despair on face.
Where to go, the rain soaks through,
His mind screams out, what can I do?
He drags his feet down the street,
Looking for somewhere dry to sleep.
He sees a doorway, but someone's there,
There isn't any room to spare.
He's soaked he's cold, his mind's gone numb,
He didn't see the lorry come.
His body chucked onto the ground,
Eye's wide open not a sound.
Rucksack spilt all on the road,
No more to be the heavy load.
His medal's shining on his chest,
At last, the soldier will find some rest.

Lindy O'Leary

The Holiday

When I was younger, about 12, we (my mum and dad and two sisters) went to Tenby on holiday. Now my dad was a big-time photographer, especially with a movie camera, and used to catch all our holidays on his then standard Super Eight movie camera.

Well, after one lovely holiday, my dad wanted to have some scenes of himself for a change, so asked my mum to film him leaving the holiday home carrying the suitcases. My mum usually struggled with learning new things, so Dad went into great detail, about what buttons to press, and how to hold it, and Mum had a go.

Dad went into the holiday home, picked up the suitcases (and they were packed) and strode towards Mum with a big smile on his face.

"Shall I start now?" said Mum, as Dad walked past her.

"Yes," said my dad "I've just done it. Never mind, I'll go back in, now you know what to do?"

"Yes Ron," said Mum.

Back in the house, my dad went with the cases with the three bemused sisters watching.

"Right," said Dad, "are you ready?"

"Yes," said Mum.

Out came Dad with a beaming smile on his face, suitcases in hand.

"Did you get that?" he said as he walked past her?"

"Which button is record?" said mum.

Dad put the suitcases down.

"That one I pointed at"

"Oh!" Said mum.

Dad picked up the suitcases again as Mum had obviously done it wrong, and went back into the house.

"Ready," said Dad,

"Ready," said Mum.

Out he came again.

"Sorry my finger slipped," said Mum.

By now, me and my sisters were doing the dying fly on the floor, we were in hysterics. Well, we did get a recording in the end as that is how I got my story but when Dad came out of the holiday home, he looked a bit haggard and was definitely not smiling.

Lindy O'Leary

The Lonely Gargoyle

High up on a church tower was a gargoyle, one of the scariest ugliest gargoyles you ever saw. But, he wasn't all bad; he was made of stone, but his heart wasn't. He was lonely way up there, with no one to talk to, looking down at the hustle and bustle of life going on down below. I could be happy if I had someone to share my life with, he thought. Years ago, he had a partner on the other side of the great tower, but time had destroyed it, and all that was left was a small pile of rubble where it once stood.

Now down below amongst the throngs of people, was this lad. He came mostly to church to laugh at the poor bedraggled people and children. His parents owned the manor, and he was their only son. He thought himself above everybody, he had a nasty character. Hitting them with his brass-handled cane if they got near him, jeering at the lame, kicking the beggars out of the way. His parents were nice people though, and very worried about the way he acted, as especially when they died, he would be lord of the manor, and they knew he would treat the people badly.

Well, one strange day (you get them sometimes)! One strange magical day something happened to stop all this, and two lives were changed forever. It was a Halloween' Sunday, and the weather was bad. The poor stood outside the church, hands stretched hoping for a few pennies to help feed their families. The Lord's coach drew up as usual, and out came the Lord and Lady followed by their son. They handed out pennies and kind words to their people, but unknown to them, their son behind them whacked a few hands with his brass-topped cane.

"Go and work, you lazy scum," he said. Well, they already did work and worked hard, but never earned enough, times were hard.

Now, one person he abused was the local medicine woman as she was known, and he really hit her hard. Well as you know another name sometimes given to a knowledgeable woman like that is a witch and she screamed and cursed.

Then she stared at him and said, "You really have a heart of stone. You may as well join them who are made of stone" and the strangest thing happened. He suddenly was gone, just disappeared. All that was left was his cane. Nobody saw what happened as the witch was last in line. His parents turned around to hurry him up and couldn't see him. They called, no answer, they came back out of the church, where was he!

They got the local people to search, they found his cane but nothing else.

They searched all day, nothing. Days went by but nothing was ever heard of him again. Very strange. But even stranger still, people noticed another gargoyle on the other side of the tower.

"Well, I'll be," they said, "Where did that come from?"

Lindy O'Leary

The Cove

Peter, Jane and Mary were excited. They were on holiday at their aunt's in Devon and they were going to the beach today, to try out their raft, which they had worked so hard on all week.

"Don't forget the picnic" said Mary, the oldest at eleven. Peter was ten and Jane was nine.

"It is in my rucksack," said Peter feeling very important, being the only boy, and feeling that he was the natural leader.

They left their aunt's cottage and walked the short distance to the beach zigzagging over the sand dunes.

"Lucky Aunty," said Peter "I wish I could always live here."

The smell of the fresh sea air wafted towards them as they got down to the beach, and there was the raft they had all worked so hard on, with the paddle safely attached. Excitedly they ran towards it. The girls got there first.

"I won," said Jane.

"That's not fair," said Peter, "The picnic kept bumping on my back, and slowed me down."

"Oh, don't be silly," said Mary,

"It wasn't a race anyhow. But I did win," said Jane coyly.

"Well, you can blooming well carry the picnic next time," said Peter, ruffled.

"Oh, stop it!" said Mary. "Jane's only winding you up, aren't you Jane?"

"Of course," said Jane, but crossed her fingers behind her back. They untied the raft.

"Look," said Peter trying to get his importance back again. "Let's ferry over to that little cove over there. It's not far and I bet there are some interesting rock pools there."

"What a good idea," said Jane, giving his status back to him, as she had had her bit of fun, and didn't want to ruin the day. They hopped on the raft, the girls sat down and Peter stood up with the big paddle, and ferried the raft along. The wind was in their favour. The sun shining, they glided along chattering and gossiping excitedly, the sun rays bouncing off the gentle ripples, the seagulls gliding and diving, screeching to each other. They reached the little cove in about ten minutes.

"That was amazing, well done Peter," said Mary.

"Yes, well done," said Jane. Peter stuck out his chest. Yes, he was the natural leader. He jumped off the raft when it was shallow enough and pulled it onto the beach. It was only a small cove, lots of interesting rock pools, and a little cave in the rock face at the back, perfect.

"Explore or picnic first?" said Mary.

"Oh picnic!" said Jane who was always hungry.

"I second that," said Peter.

So, they sat on the beach and got stuck in. Homemade lemonade Aunty had made, plum cake and thick cheese wedge sandwiches.

"That was great," said Peter.

"Yes," said Mary and Jane. "Aunty certainly knows how to do a picnic, let's look around now."

They explored the many rock pools, seeing the crabs scuttling off and the little fish darting this way and that quickly as the children's shadows alerted them that something was there. Peter left the girls and walked towards the little cove. It was cooler there. He went inside, it was a bit scary, but he was a boy, what did he care. He went a little further in. There he saw a big rock pool. Wow, he thought, I'll have to show this to the girls. He got down on his knees and peered into it. It was so clear he could almost see his reflection, but hey that was strange, he peered closer, and that didn't look anything like him, it must be the ripples or something, or his eyes playing tricks in this light.

He went to turn around to shout to the girls when this icy pair of arms stretched out from the pool and pulled him in so quickly, that he had no time to scream or struggle and dragged him under. The thing or creature which now had strangely taken on Peter's appearance, stepped out of the pool and walked towards the cave entrance.

"Mary, Jane, come here. You have to see this," said Peter.

Lindy O'Leary

Illustrations by Dona Allen

175

The Old Bookshop

The bookshop had been there years, since the street had been built. It looked quirky, no-one had tried to modernise it. It stood at the corner of the street, looking almost dark and foreboding. The ancient shop had kept its character, time had moved on but not in the bookshop.

Jack stood outside, pensively. He had been searching for a long time – could it be in here? He pressed his nose to the window, he couldn't see much, just a few books on view, not even modern ones, no advertising leaflets, weirdly, more stuffed animals than anything staring back at you. Yes, very unusual almost, foreboding, the lifeless badger seemed to say, "If you come in here, you'll end up like me."

There wasn't anything to really draw you in except curiosity. You wouldn't know it was a bookshop, if the sign wasn't above, more like a taxidermist place. Should he, shouldn't he? It was silly feeling nervous, it was a hot sunny day, he had come down to Cornwall on holiday, well a bit of a quest really, like all his holidays. He was an anthophile and he was after information on a certain flower that he had found years ago but had never found in any book yet. He had always loved flowers since he was a child. The other children at school took the mickey out of him, he didn't mind, he was too busy to mind. Every day after school he would be out in the fields or woods, searching, listing all he could find, but there had been this one flower, only one, and he knew nothing about it. He had it carefully pressed, it had almost taken over himself.

How many book shops now? Well (he laughed) it's certainly broadened my horizon on holidays, I could write a book on that alone. There must be some information somewhere, it can't be the only one in the world. He pushed the door open, a bell jangled.

He had to adjust his eyes. It was quite dark and musty in there, must be the smell from the dead animals. He gave a shudder and walked towards the counter at the end. There was no-one there, but an old-fashioned bell that you pressed was on the table, he pressed it.

A wizardly old man seemed to come from nowhere, quite sharpish. "Yes".

Jack stared at him. Why he must be almost as old as the shop!

"I wonder if you have any old books on flowers," Jack said.

"I have many books young man, you need to be more specific," said the old man.

"Well," said Jack, as he handed over his precious package, "I am trying to find out about this". The old man carefully removed the tissue paper from the pressed flower. Jack noticed a hint of recognition in his face.

"You do! Don't you?" said Jack excitedly.

"Yes," said the old man just as excited, "Many years ago, and yes, I do have some information in a book, a very old book. Now where did I put it? Sit down sir, I need to go in the back and search. Here have a nice cold glass of lemonade while you're waiting, it's warm out there today, and you must be feeling hot."

Jack sat down. At last, years and years of searching, now finally. He knocked back the lemonade, that felt good. Suddenly he felt a bit weak, strange, must be all that excitement. He seemed to be floating. Next thing he knew, he was staring out the shop window, how can that be, he felt very strange, he couldn't move.

He heard a voice, it said "I told you so." It seemed to come from the stuffed badger opposite him. Jack could see his, or what seemed to be his reflection staring back. How could that be, he was looking directly at a mirror image of a ferret. The old man stepped back admiring his handiwork. "Well, he should have been a stoat but that will do nicely," he smiled.

Lindy O'Leary

New Beginnings

She had had enough. The years of all that farting, snoring, and coughing, and that unwashed smell. Enough. She wanted to live her life now. She had given him 40 years, running around after him, doing his bidding, picking up his pants and socks, if she had never, they would have been knee deep in them. He had been all right in the beginning, most men were. But men were like hills. You start at the peak and slowly roll down. Her small bag was packed. She had filled the freezer with all the rubbish he liked. Chips, pies, pizzas, and of course, he knew where the chip shop was and the pub. She shuddered to think of him wading through all those rancid socks and pants when she was gone, but hey, without her to remind him to change, there probably wouldn't be so many.

The floor upstairs creaked. The toilet with its usual loud acceptance of the night before flushed. He came downstairs heavily.

"Morning darling," he smiled. "Tea ready?"

"Just putting the kettle on dear," she said.

He went and sat down in the living room as usual. She picked up her case, put her hat on, and quietly shut the door behind her.

Lindy O'Leary

Ghost Story

Rosemary wrote the first two paragraphs of this and set the challenge of completing the story. Lindy rose to the challenge..

The house sat on the top of the hill, its crumbling Georgian frontage looking imperiously down on the small Devon village below. Separated by a steep lane, the old house was linked to the village by the equally old church and churchyard which lay in between. The house and the garden had seen better days. The garden boasted a good crop of dandelions, nettles, and brambles. The latter however did yield a good crop of fruit every year. Big juicy blackberries to die for. Ro and Darren had gratefully accepted the chance to rent the top half of the big old house. It was close to their new jobs and very spacious. It was the mid 70's, and jobs and flats were hard to come by.

The bottom floor included the Elizabethan kitchen and the outhouse. They were out of bounds as it was occupied by the elderly landlady, who was there most of the time, she assured them. Very occasionally, Lavinia Freeman-Hawe explained, she would spend the night with friends in the village. It would be good to know that there would be someone to keep an eye on things. She didn't bother to mention the small fact that there was somebody else already there.

There it was again, a clangy sort of rumbly noise. Ro was getting frustrated. She had looked forward to this bath. She had lit all the candles, which gave it a dreamy look, and bought some very expensive bath oil, which she normally wouldn't spend that much on.

She wanted to inject a bit of oomph into their relationship. Since the move, Darren seemed to have got complacent, he didn't seem as attentive as he used to be when they lived in London. Well, it was more exciting there true, parties all the time, people popping in for drinks, but surely their relationship was built on more than that. She thought, maybe they would even be moving onto the next level, marriage, children.

But the way things were going lately, she'd be lucky! She could see herself ending up like that lonely old crank downstairs. No, things had to change starting from now.

That bloody tap. Tonight, of all nights. Why wasn't the water coming out? Darren would be home soon and the whole idea would be ruined. Miss

Freeman-Hawe would be out tonight. Well, out of bounds or not, she would have to go downstairs to look at the plumbing, to see if there was anything she could do (or hit) to get the darn thing working.

She pulled her dressing gown tight around her, as Lavinia wasn't over generous with the heating, and made her way downstairs.

Just to make sure she knocked loudly on the door.

"Miss Freeman-Hawe, could I have a word please?"

Nothing, she tried again. Nope, she wasn't in. She would have heard her, as her hearing was annoyingly good, especially when they were playing records. The door wasn't locked. She opened it.

Ro cautiously walked in.

"Hello! Miss Freeman-Hawe!" Getting louder she walked straight in.

It hadn't been decorated since the 1920s at least. It was like walking back in time. The old wind-up gramophone (no wonder she didn't like their one), the low leather furniture, the hideous chunky walnut sideboard, and the carpet, it was like some weird hopscotch game. It had so many patches in it.

The Tiffany lights gave the room a garish look, though she could see it was polished and looked after, but she bet she didn't hoover, she couldn't it would gobble up the rest of the carpet. On the sideboard was a silver-framed photo. She went closer. NO!! that couldn't be Lavinia. It was of a beautiful girl. Long tumbling dark hair to her shoulders stylishly fixed, slim, wearing a long flowing slinky dress, staring up adoringly to a very handsome gentleman dressed accordingly so. He wasn't looking at her, he was staring straight ahead. But those eyes, they looked cold, even evil, he made her shudder.

She was suddenly startled, the door slammed, and there stood Miss Freeman-Hawe.

"How dare you? What are you doing here in my home?" said Lavinia.

"Oh sorry!" Ro said, "I came looking for you. The waters not working in the bathroom."

"It does not give you the right to walk in my private quarters after specifically being asked not to," said Lavinia.

"Well, I was planning a special night, you know how it is", replied Ro as she nodded towards the photo.

"Yes, I know how it is," Lavinia said under her breath.

"But the hot water is not coming through, so I came down here to see if you could help. I know the plumbing plays up now and then and thought maybe it could be sorted out quickly. Is that you? You look lovely, and he is very handsome. Were you married?" said Ro hoping to diffuse the situation.

Lavinia went over to the sideboard and slammed the photo facedown.

"That's none of your business! You've no right to come in my room and look at my things, no right at all." Lavinia looked furious. "As for planning special nights, they aren't worth it, none of them are worth it."

"I'm sorry, I didn't mean to pry," said Ro "I just really needed to get the plumbing working. I'm sorry if things didn't work out for you." This seemed to annoy Lavinia even more.

"Who said they didn't!" Lavinia said. "Still prying, interfering, why can't people mind their own business? Well, if you must, the plumbing is down here." She opened a door, which Ro hadn't noticed, so cleverly concealed in the gaudy wallpaper, that you would not have known it was there. Stairs led down. Of course, a house this age would have a cellar.

Lavinia took a candleholder from the sideboard and lit the candle in it. Then she started to descend the stairs. Ro followed nervously behind, it smelt awful. Don't know about the plumbing being down here, she thought, more like a septic tank. They got down to the bottom when Lavinia said, "Oh I forgot the spanner, you take the candle, I know the way back up all right. I ought to," she said under her breath.

Ro took the candle, and Lavinia went back up the stairs, rather nimbly for a woman of her age, she thought. She looked around holding the candle up. Oh, that smell, what was it, surely not rats. She heard a noise, something large moved in the corner, and she moved the candle nearer. Then she saw it, him, those eyes. She would recognise them anywhere, they didn't look so arrogant now, but still cold, and evil. Suddenly she heard the voice of Lavinia.

"You can have him!" Lavinia shouted. "I know you've come back for him; I recognised you the moment you walked through my door. Well, he's not the looker he was."

"What are you saying?" Ro shouted, "You're mad."

"No, I am not, I knew you wouldn't give up. You ruined my life years ago. That photo was taken on my engagement, my special night. Did you wonder why he didn't come back to you? Did you wait long?" Lavinia laughed hideously and madly. "Well, he's all yours now. Don't know what I ever saw in him. Oh! You can have the house too. I suspect that was the plan, the reason, my money."

The door slammed and as the candle dimmed the last thing Ro saw was those cold grey eyes coming closer.

Darren hoped Miss Freeman-Hawe had passed on the phone call that he wouldn't be home tonight. That special deal on the engagement ring was worth the trip to London, but those bloody trains were so unreliable, that he would have to stay the night. It was still worth working all that overtime for, no wonder he was always tired, the size of that diamond would put a smile on her face, it would all be worth it.

The fire brigade said the fire had started in the bathroom, candles had caught the curtains, and it had spread quickly, but there were three dead bodies. Two in the basement and one in the bathroom. Who was the third body? Strange. The house was just left derelict, people avoided it. It had an air about it. Some said they heard voices, screams, and crying, but that was probably just the wind rustling through the very overgrown brambles.

Lindy O'Leary

The Care Worker

She hurries here, she hurries there,
with not a moment at work to spare
Confused faces all around,
Her feet feel like they miss the ground

Another door, another cry
She needs to go, she can't walk by
"Help me! Help me!, where's my Jim?"
She turns and sighs and then goes in.

Another day, so many faces
Their bodies there, their minds in places,
Life before, when they were young
And they could get their own things done.

Some just stare into space,
They don't want to leave that place
When they were young and free to roam
Instead of bed-bound in a home.

They call, she comes and does her best,
And then goes on to help the rest.
Once more she hears that call again
Already forgotten she has come.

There are some moments, there are some fun,
When mind and body becomes one.
A cheery smile, a memory shared
Knowing how she has helped and cared.

Always smiling always giving
Trying to make their lives worth living.
At home she sits and rubs her feet
Five minutes later she's asleep.

Linda O'Leary

Spring

All of a sudden where there was none,
A new life has just begun.
A piece of dirt so bleak and bare,
You look again there's something there.
The tiny newborn sleepy head
Rises from his winter bed.
Look again there comes another,
First his sister, now his brother.
How can that be the ground so hard.
They slip through like they're made of lard.
For months now they have been asleep,
But through their covers they now peep.
"It is time, it is time, the sun does shine".
And now the world again is mine.

Lindy O'Leary

Goodbye Summer

Heads down colour fading,
Better days left behind.
Winter's coming, they're not wanted,
Life can be so unkind.

Once in splendour, the hanging baskets
The gardener's love and pride.
Ripped from the only home they've known
And simply chucked aside.

Then taken from their old abode
In the compost bin they go.
But with old mother nature's magic
They help with next year's show.

Lindy O'Leary

L.O'L.

Graham Vaughan

My name is Graham Vaughan. I have been a member of the Liden Writers' Group for about a year. I've always enjoyed trying to write stories and poetry. A few years ago I wrote a book about my experiences of travelling through Africa in the 1970s. It was based on my journals of the time. I found that I enjoyed the process of writing and wanted to do more.

Six years ago I was diagnosed with Parkinson's and began taking medication. People often say that this type of medication can bring about more creativity in the people who take it. My creativity took the form of music and poetry. A lot of my poems are about the condition and how it affects me; however, I now want to move on and write about other things. The group has helped me to do this as we often choose a random subject to write about.

I hope you enjoy my contributions.

This Chair

This was written following Parkinson's diagnosis.

This chair rests in the pool of light thrown down by the standard lamp placed behind it.

This chair sits high backed, wooden footed and winged.

This chair has a stain high up the back where young men, now old, have sat Brylcreemed, leaving their mark.

This chair is where I can see the pictures on the glass cabinet.

Shiny faced grandchildren in clean crisp uniforms beaming into the camera.

One boy standing proudly with one boot atop a football, his mates with arms around shoulders, medals shining, looking grown up.

This chair is where I smile and weep, sit and sleep, yawn and ache, fake a smile when I want to cry.

This chair is where I noticed my cup begin to rattle in its saucer, I held my arm but still it rattled.

This chair is where I try to relax when the tremor grows and anxiety attacks.

I sit in this chair and think of others who tremor and go on this journey too.

And I'll smile because I'm not alone.

Graham Vaughan - 2022

Non-Verbal

This was written following Parkinson's diagnosis, regarding fear of losing the power of speech.

When my voice is quiet and I have words that are not heard.

How will I be understood when the sound I make is slurred?

When I hear someone speak, expressing views I do not share,

Will my speech just dissipate, lost in great nowhere?

Will my thoughts be seen as nothing with no contribution for debate?

Will I sit in silence, mute, getting more and more irate?

How will I cope when there seems no hope, and I want to be upbeat and bright?

My mind playing tricks, thinking thoughts I can't fix

Eyes wide-awake in the night.

Graham Vaughan - 2024

The Face

The room was silent as if holding its breath until the quietest sigh, almost beyond the range of hearing, uttered from her mouth.

Her black hair seemed to hide a frown, a headache maybe but the dark fringe seemed to hide that from the viewer.

Her thin lipped mouth flat lined across her face like a heart monitor after death, ashen and pale.

Her eyes were as if weary of life, they would linger too long, not looking but staring past her vicinity into a distant place. A memory maybe, not one that she wished to re-call but one that insisted on being recalled uninvited.

Her head turned almost imperceptibly, just enough for the light to shorten the shadows of her eyebrows and nose. The heavy wrinkles and lines of her face now showing the imperfection of what had long since been perfect.

Her eyelids rose slowly and those pale eyes scanned the room searching for some reason to rest and find comfort.

What had this woman been through, what horrors had caused her expression to be so?

There was an untold story in this face that needed to be heard. Her lips parted slightly as if to speak but then slowly closed keeping that story locked away. Then the eyelids closed as slowly as if in collaboration with the mouth to deny any hint of the secret to escape.

"CUT!" a voice rang out. "Brilliant my darling, absolutely brilliant!" called the director as he jumped out of his chair. "How does she do it?" He questioned as he turned to the film crew. "Well done lighting too absolutely first class."

A young girl approached the chair where the woman sat. "Can I get you anything madam, a tea or a drink perhaps?'

"No," she snapped unnecessarily harshly, "just get make up to take these wrinkles off before I am deformed by them forever."

"Right away Miss Coleman." the girl said as she withdrew backwards into the darkness of the studio behind the cameras.

Graham Vaughan - 2023

Today's The Day

Today's the day I feel it in my bones

The day I stop all the moans and groans

Positive Mental Attitude, that's me,

The day looks good as far as I can see

I may go for a run, or cycle on my bike

Make a pack up lunch and go for a hike

I'll get sponsored and walk a very long way

That's how good I feel today.

I'll get creative and play my guitar

Get on the telly and be a star

They'll say he's amazing, he's found a cure

He's got PD you know, are you sure?

He used to walk funny and shuffle around

Sometimes he'd stop still like he was stuck to the ground

But now he's a dancer, so light on his feet

He's turning heads as he skips down the street

But you all know what's coming, it's not as it seems

It was all in his head, just vivid dreams

It was nice as it lasted just for a while

At least when he woke he was wearing a smile

So on days when he wakes and is wanting to weep

One thing he can try is to just go back to sleep!

Graham Vaughan - 2023

Rolph And The Red Nose

"As with all medical procedures, there is a certain element of risk," the surgeon said. "The main one is infection, but it is below 3% for this procedure. So no cause for concern there. We need you to sign a consent form then we're good to go."

The cost of the procedure was £2000 and Rolph had taken advantage of the special low interest loan to pay for the cosmetic surgery.

"Good, the payment has gone through, that's all in order now so we just need you to look at the colour pallet and choose the shade of red. Then we can complete everything." Rolph chose a bright cherry red that he thought would really stand out.

"This is quite an unusual request, but it is easily 'doable' if you know what I mean. You'll only need a local anaesthetic." The surgeon chatted; he seemed confident.

An hour later Rolph was looking in the mirror to see his new look; he was pleased with outcome. The bulbous tip of his nose was a fine bright Crimson red. It stood out, proudly contrasting with his pale, white-washed complexion. He left the surgery and stepped out in the daylight, expecting admiring glances from passers by .

People did not respond in the way he expected! There were giggles and some stifled laughter, but no admiring looks. Did they not know it is Red Nose Day in a week? By the time he got home, he was hiding his nose behind his scarf.

His family was shocked that he had gone ahead with his idea; his brothers were particularly fascinated. They thought he had been joking when he had talked about it. He tried to justify his actions by saying he would raise money by being a personality on social media and making public appearances.

His brothers thought they would arrange a prank to embarrass him by inviting a TV reporter to the house to interview him. The idea was to humiliate him.

Rolph had no idea when he opened the door that he would be met by a TV crew, and his face went almost a deeper red than his nose. The brothers looked on as the interview started, they were silently giggling in the background. The TV reporter thrust the microphone forward and said, "Tell us why you did this, what possessed you to actually change the colour of your nose permanently?"

"I thought that I could help make Red Nose Day special by making it more real, but it hasn't done that has it?" He looked despondent," I really wanted to be taken seriously and to be a stand-up comedian one day. But I've ended up making an idiot of myself."

The brothers looking on amazed when the reporter said that she thought it was a wonderful and brave thing to do. To take the risk of being ridiculed in order to raise awareness of the cause was a fantastic thing to do.

She picked up her phone and speed dialled a number. "Hi Lenny darling, I think I've found the new face for Red Nose Day!"

Soon Rolph was being invited as a guest on talk shows, to open supermarkets, cut ribbons to open new businesses, being pictured digging with new shovels into the ground to start a new social housing project and raising millions for good causes. He donated any payments and always picked events that benefited in the spirit of Red Nose Day. To bring positive change to those disadvantaged around the world and the UK.

The craze of having a Red Nose by cosmetic surgery had caught on and people were having the procedure done and then using social media to support good causes around the world.

Rolph was very happy with the way things turned out. Commentators said that it seemed a whole new approach to helping others and the feeling was spreading that we can change things for the better.

Meanwhile the Harley Street surgeon was booked up for months ahead. A red nose cosmetic procedure was now £5000 and people were having it done in their droves. It had become a symbol of how much people cared.

The surgeon was also pleased with the way things had turned out! He stood and looked out between procedures to admire his shiny new Bentley parked outside the surgery.

Some things never change!

Graham Vaughan - 2024

Learning How Not To Drive
(Subtitle: Life in the bus lane!)

You can't drive anymore the consultant said,
There's something wrong with that thing in yer head
It's shanks's pony for you as you go
So get used to it now and take things slow
Chill out man, don't make a fuss
Have you ever thought of taking the bus?
You're the age that you can get a free pass
So travel the highways in style and class
Good idea me thinks, I'll download the app
To tell me which bus, don't get in a flap
Bus number three at a quarter past
Will get me there, and really fast!
I look at my watch it's almost time
I stand with the others in the line
Here it comes, I see the bus slowing
But it's not number three where I am going!
It's a number seven it says on the bus
The folks in the line say "oh that'll be us
So I'm left all alone, just my app and me
It's not as easy I as thought it would be.
I'm despondent and late, and all on my own
So reluctantly I get out my phone.
I'm sorry, I say to my long suffering wife
Could you come pick me up and save my life!

Graham Vaughan - 2023

The Quilt

Every square we knitted told the story of us,
Early the squares were knitted fast and with lust.
Bright colours, yellows and blues and greens.
Each square sat neatly with the next it seemed.
Then over the years it started to wear
It showed signs of neglect, worn and threadbare.
The colour became dull, the stitches more loose.
It lay lifeless, where in the past it used to seduce.
Colours, darker and careless, more stitches undone.
The squares were uneven, threads missing, un-spun.
Our quilt was put away in the cupboard for now
We'd always meet to repair it somehow
There came a time when we forgot who we were
She'd say it was me, I'd say it was her.
As we split our possessions, what's yours and what's mine?
We found our quilt and remembered that time.
So you looked in the cupboard, found some spare wool,
Repaired a few gaps and made them full.
We sat in silence you held the quilt to your face.
Tears ran down our cheeks, leaving their trace.
We began knitting together our stitches entwined
Reopened the boxes of what's yours and what's mine?
Now our quilt continues to grow.
Some times it grows fast and some times it's slow.
But it now covers our bed, we know what we've built.
Our lifetime together in the form of a quilt.

Graham Vaughan - 2024

The Village Hall

I like to support my village hall.

Lots goes on there. I've seen it all.

I've been to the annual flower show

And seen how big Fred's turnips grow.

I haven't been to the weight loss class.

I've given the philosophy class a pass.

There was a time when I country danced?

Just the beginners, not the advanced.

Dog shows,

Keep fitters, Scouts, and even Cubs

Have been caught sneaking out to the local pub.

I've given blood there, cleared the car park of mud.

And put flowers in the bedding, to make it nice for a wedding

When the fella from the big house, we called him Jake,

Went and died, the hall was where we held his wake.

I didn't go to the Women's Institute bake.

But I went to Tantric yoga, big mistake!

I glimpsed Mrs. Smith and the man half her age having a cuddle at the back

of the stage

It's where all the action is in our quiet place.

But sometimes our village shows its other face.

Competition sometimes goes too far

When the judging standard is not up to par.

Leaving bitterness and jealousy within our normally quiet community

But in the summer everyone's happy, everyone's fine.

At the village fete in the warm sunshine.

I like it that we have the village hall and

I'm very glad it's there for the use of us all!

Graham Vaughan

Feeling Christmassy

Christmassy - adjective, informal. As in "A tree completed the Christmassy feel".

Do you know what that Christmassy feeling is? It's hard to describe, to pin down exactly how it feels. An excitement, feeling of anticipation, maybe an impatience for something different from the norm? To some it may be aroused by seeing the Christmas lights go on in the High-street, to others it may be hearing carols sung in Church, others will see the shops stocked with Christmas goodies.

For me, the first time I felt Christmassy that I can remember was in the larder at home when I was 8 or 9 years old! Having a sneaky look for something to eat I glimpsed, behind the flour bin on the floor at the back of the larder, large tins of fruit cocktail and peach slices.

Over the following weeks I would peek and see the stash grow, adding things such as glacè cherries, nuts, candied peel and custard powder. I knew these to be the ingredients for the Christmas trifle! Every time I sneaked a look I would feel that Christmassy feeling!

It was in the early 1950s, ration books were still in use and families were used to managing food on a budget. Money was tight but there were ways to put something by each week for special occasions.

I started to know that something was happening when the world I knew changed for a few weeks. I then began to associate that time with presents, lights on a tree, laughter and food. Over the years that special feeling was triggered by the simplest of things like going into the loft to find the boxes of decorations. It was a dusty dark place, with spiders' webs that would brush your face. It was worth that discomfort though to get the boxes down and open them to see the sparkling tree decorations, baubles and streamers.

There was an impatience about every aspect of the lead-up to Christmas. Opening the first window of the advent calendar at the beginning of December it seemed a long time before Christmas Eve and it seemed they were designed to keep you in suspense! Amongst the decorations there are some I remember vividly. A brass ornament with four angels balanced on a kind of a merry-go-round that would spin when small candles were lit beneath them. They caught the light and it bounced around the ceiling and the walls

That Christmassy feeling is harder now to re-create 70 years later, as I become more cynical, but I can still see it in children's eyes today. My mother told me years later that she knew I always looked for the tinned peaches in the larder! So long after it was no longer a secret, she kept the tradition going. Unspoken, silently she placed tins of peaches and fruit cocktail in the larder behind the flour bin, knowing it would remind me of that Christmassy ritual.

Happy Christmas to mums everywhere!

Graham Vaughan

Christmas At The Chemist

The pharmacy in my dad's chemist shop was a busy place in December, with all the colds and flu remedies having to be dispensed. Prescriptions hanging from bulldog clips in neat rows. The dispensers efficiently reaching for packets and bottles, counting them out. Handwriting labels, trying to understand the doctor's scribbles. The medication is placed on the prescription ready for the pharmacist, my dad, to check. Customers waiting patiently for their name to be called to collect their medicines. My dad hoping they would see something in the shop to buy while they were waiting

The whole family helped – mum, my brother and me. Dad would sometimes get grumpy, all the long hours standing in the dispensary he looked tired and didn't seem very Christmassy.

The shop also sold cosmetics, hair colour and over-the-counter medicines, shampoo etc. Some time earlier in the autumn the reps from companies such as Yardley, Mornay, Revlon and Coty would come into the shop to take the orders for Christmas gift sets. They had all their products presented in glossy brochures. Dad would negotiate with the reps to get the best price and quantities of these gift sets. It was common for these sales reps to offer gifts if he bought a certain amount. So a set of sherry glasses or maybe even a hostess trolley if you ordered enough cases.

Dad wasn't interested in any gifts and would give the reps a hard time if he felt he wasn't getting the best deal! "I don't want any of your gifts, I want a case discount!" I once heard him say loudly. I bet they dreaded coming to "Vaughans the Chemist".

The moment came when the stock arrived and we made space on the counters for the gift sets and a big display in the window with fake snow and everything seemed very festive. The newsagents across the road started to display large boxes of chocolates with pictures on the front of Christmas scenes and the hardware shop had its first trees out. At the age of eleven I wasn't too old to still feel the thrill of anticipation.

The cheapest gift sets were about five shillings. (At this point I should point out to you youngsters! One pound was 20 shillings, so therefore 10 shillings would be 50p) For that you would get a bar of soap and a tin of talcum powder in a fancy box. The sets then ranged upwards from there to 12/6* to

15/6 and some at 17/6! These more expensive sets would have bath salts or even perfume. Every time a gift set over the value of five shillings was sold, the member of staff could record it in a book countersigned by my dad. Then on Christmas Eve the total for each member of staff was added up and a bonus given to the staff member who had sold the most. Of course at the age of eleven, I worked mostly in the stock room. I had very little chance of winning. However there was always one special gift set that stood out and was priced, I seem to remember, at 25/- (£1.25p). To sell this gift set attracted a bonus on its own!

One Christmas Eve all staff were gathered in the dispensary having a glass of sherry and mum was working out who was to get the bonus. The 25/- gift set had not sold that year and was destined to be split up and the items put into stock. Before he started speaking to the staff, dad asked me to go and put the latch on the shop door, hang up the "closed" sign and turn the lights down. Just as I was putting the closed sign up a man pushed the door, he was panting from running. So I opened the door slightly and said that we were closed. He put his foot in the door and pleaded with me: "I'm desperate" he said, "I haven't got my wife anything for Christmas and you're my last hope, do you not have any gift sets left?"

I said, "We've only got the very expensive one – it's 25 shillings!" Without hesitation he said through the half open door, "I'll take it!" So I made a decision and opened the door to let him in. He took out his wallet, pulled out a pound note then rustled in his pocket, found two half crowns. He thanked me profusely, grabbed his gift set and said I'd saved his life. He went away very happy. When I returned to the dispensary Dad scolded me for letting a customer in after he'd told me to shut the shop. "I heard the till ring," dad said. "What did that fellow want?"

In reply, I said with pride, "He wanted the big gift set, so I sold it to him!" (I wasn't really supposed to ring up anything more than 5/- without a member of staff present!) That should mean I get the bonus but Dad started to say it was a contest for the staff and not the family.

But the staff clapped; one sales assistant said that it was a good job I had let him in! The staff all went quiet. My mum threw my dad one of her looks and he softened! He could see he was becoming the Scrooge in this scenario and he relented. I got two shillings! Maureen, the senior staff member, said well done and gave me a hug.

We had a good Christmas and when Dad opened the shop door on the first day after the holiday there was a note from the chap who bought the 25/- present for his wife, thanking us profusely! Dad gave me the note to keep and I still have it now!

Happy Christmas to all shop staff!

Graham Vaughan Nov 2024

* *12/6 is a way of denoting 12 shillings and 6 pence – pre-decimalisation*

Staying Alive

Rather be alive than not, rather remembered than forgot.

Rather exist than be a ghost, rather be me than just almost.

If I could choose in life to win or lose.

They are both the same when you're confused.

So I'll stand up straight and carry on.

I'll stay here, dare the demons be gone.

Sometimes I may feel differently.

Sometimes I'll feel more like me.

And find a reason to believe,

So I'll choose to stay and not to leave.

Graham Vaughan - 2024

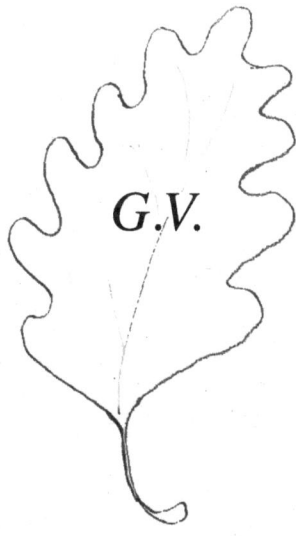

Jenny Weeks

Jenny from Liden Writers' Group, the next eldest of the bunch, I'm Swindon born and bred. I started writing about 30 years ago a story of my family, then was encouraged to join and expand, with help from the group and Radio Swindon 105.5. I write for fun. I like to make people smile.

TV

Aaagh! I'm watching TV.

What's wrong with me?

It's a load of rubbish, mostly what I see.

People not payin' their rent on time;

People in a mess – I'm glad it's not mine.

People with no clothes on – what's that about?

Showin' their bits off – "Cover up!" I shout.

A vet with his hand right up a cow's bum;

Valuables I don't have selling for a princely sum;

Day after day, murder, mystery and mayhem.

Police series showing felons and some like 'em.

News full of misery, weather the same.

When is the news going to be cheerful again?

Ha! That was a joke! But some good news please.

Love Island – what's that about? She's really a tease!

Bachelor looking for a bride – yeah, right!

They all finish up with a girlie fight.

The soaps are rubbish. I still watch some.

So much intrigue. I know, unpleasant things to come.

Give me a romance, including kids and dogs;

Maybe some mystery, mists lying, and fogs,

To cover the ground as the heroine runs,

As the felon chases them and the hero comes.

But just – a little bit of nonsense please!

Jenny Weeks - 2024

Updated Nursery Rhymes

Humpty Dumpty

Why did Humpty Dumpty sit on that wall?
Humpty Dumpty knew it would fall!
The wall was leaning over but he just wanted fame;
He smiled at the camera again and again.
Jumping up he posed – 'cause he could.
Laughingly he wobbled – not that he should!
As over he went with a crash, with the wall.
Photographers said, "Not good – not at all!"
All the paparazzi and all of the men
Couldn't put that silly egg together again.

The Old Woman Who Lived in a Shoe

Where is that old woman who lived in that shoe?
The one with the children, didn't know what to do.
You know – the one who slapped them and put them to bed.
She's in prison for child abuse now, they said.

Three Blind Mice

They could not really run;
The farmer's wife had cut off their legs for fun.
Along with their tails – they couldn't steer;
Don't think they'll live long, I fear.

Two Fat Pigeons

Two fat pigeons sitting in a row;
One named Fred one named Flo.
Fly away Freddie, Fly away Flo
Come back Fred, Flo's a no go !!!!

Jenny Weeks - 2024

Who Am I Now?

The topic for the week was 'mental health'. How would I feel?

I walked in a cloud of pain and despair, thinking and wondering exactly what had happened in my world. It had changed so much. My life was methodical, neat, happy. All blown out of the water, my mind a blur. Then out of my chaotic thoughts, occasionally comes a clear thought, only to be clouded again by pain and anguish. Me fighting to recover it again and make sense of it. How did it happen? When did it change? I can't remember clearly enough to make sense of that at all at the moment.

The envy I feel grows at times into a hard green jealousy right into my soul. What was I lacking? What could have changed? I was not strong enough to fight them. He's gone now with my child. I just wander on my own. Sad, lonely, waiting for my next pill. I will get well I'm sure, with time and care but the doubtful feelings still remain.

I'm not losing my mind, am I?

Oh. Here are the visitors. There's a man and a child coming.

"Hello" I say. "Who are you?"

Jenny Weeks - 2024

Life At Home

Move your head my man said to me
He couldn't see round me at the TV you see
Cuddle up he says. I do. Very me.
But he sleeps, comfort blanket me you see.
Just resting my eyes, the first words he says
Was not asleep, grunting awake, eyes a-glaze
I've been left with the football!
Heard it all he said
I'm not tired now says he. You go to bed.
But I'm not tired, not one little bit.
Smiling, he thinks it funny me having a fit!

Illustrated by Dona Allen

Jenny Weeks - 2020

The Worm

If I was a worm what would I do
No-one knows what worms go through
They slide through the mud eating dirt on the way
Passing it through the body, what can I say?
Poor little things, the earth they turn
After all it's just a little worm
Stuck on a fork when gardens are dug
Peeled off and thrown, not even a hug
Another thing no sex for this guy
Sexless I'm told.
Ask nature WHY?

Illustrated by Dona Allen

Jenny Weeks - 2020

Fruit And Veg ... What!

This to me was not amusing or was it?

Five a day the experts say
But me, at least, come on no way
Then 7 they say, out of the blue
I really do not know what to do
Imagine 7 a day x 7 a week oh dear
Cannot see it happening now I fear
Multiply those bits of fruit and veg
Well I think I should really try and pledge
But from 49 x 4 a month really not funny
Who has the money or a strong enough tummy

Illustrated by Dona Allen

Jenny Weeks - 2024

I Sit Thinking

The smallest room, the room with a view
I sit and contemplate things to do
Whose birthday is next, what shopping I need
Not that I have many people to feed
I think of what I haven't, then what I have
All this daydreaming sat on the Lav!!

Jenny - 2024

What Gender

Talking as a group discussing topics but, as usual, I went off on my own.

I picked up a toy the other day
Is this for girl or for a boy? I say
This gender thing is getting me down
Will it make them smile or maybe frown
What if a boy does have a doll?
Dad says it may change him very droll
A girl cannot have a football
Girls do not play footie at all
Well we know that isn't true
Some parents get in such a stew
A boy pushing a doll's pram a joy
A girl kicking a ball, does not make her a boy
We are what we are in this funny old life
What we want is happy, life with no strife
To be free, to love, free to be
Gender aside, we are all people you see………..

Jenny Weeks - 2024

Illustrated by Dona Allen

What A Morning!!!!

Such a true story – such a trauma!

I am really fed up, what can I do
After all the problems I've been through
The boiler packed up, dripped through the ceiling
At 4 in the morning, comatose, wet feeling
Water dripped down my back, didn't compute
Well 4 in the morning, I'm not so astute
But by 7 three hours later, oh my stars, pours
Dripped through the ceiling for hours,
Wet everywhere it's an insurance job
So off to the loft I go, start to sob
The flipping boiler was obviously leaking
So phone emergency, to him I am speaking
Please help me quickly I say in a panic
Do not want the ceiling down, now I'm manic
Now madam do not worry, the man said to me
We will be out between 12-2 as fast as can be
Ha well you guessed, it was 2 on the clock
Always last minute, now please make it stop
He switched off the boiler, said now it's all done!!!
No heat or hot water, till tomorrow O bum!
Now he has to check if they'll pay the invoice
I have paperwork, do not think there is a choice
In the saga of this story comes the reckoning
Even at 4 put a bucket out, even if bed is beckoning…

Jenny Weeks - 2024

The Flower

The words we were given for inspiration were 'flower', 'moonlight', 'painting',,,

I walked the path in silence looked up and saw the stars
Dreaming of the time we had no worries or wars
Still dreaming, I found my way back home
Shadows and moonbeams time had flown
Set by the fire, my easel and paint ready for me
A flame of inspiration spilling over for all to see
I feverishly started on my portraits of a flower
A single snowdrop under a tree, oh the power
It gave me, with moonbeams slanting through the trees
Beholding my flower dancing in the breeze.
To put on canvas, the vision was hard to find,
Stop, now to put my training to practice soon
Start with the backdrop, darkness and the moon
So moonbeams will pass through trees to snowdrop
It will glow in my painting, trees a backdrop
This little flower pure and white half open for me
Night flies dancing in moonlight shaft I see
But my hands do not comply or help at all
If I start tonight, I'm heading for a fall
So maybe tomorrow when my mind is stilled
The picture I have dreamed of will be fulfilled....

Jenny Weeks - 2024

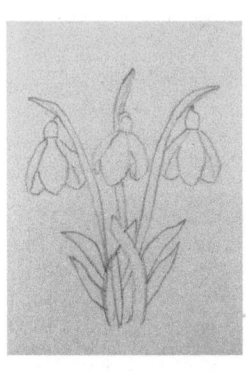

Illustrated by Dona Allen

Baking my Way…

Never could make a beautifully risen cake, why?

Today I have been trying to bake a cake
Maybe I should not have stayed in to bake
My cakes are a mystery, they very rarely rise
Never had much praise, never won a prize,
My daughter laughs when my cakes come out
They've sunk again! and did she shout
With glee that is, she is a very good cook
But, my cakes taste good, who cares how they look
I fill up the middle with cream and or sweets
The children love it, Nan it's full of treats
They say as they tuck into more and more
Laughing and stuffed as they go out the door
Discussing my cakes and laughing with pleasure
Now you see I've that memory to treasure
So the laughs on them as they mock my baking
My Memories…. I smile and put another cake in ….
NannaJen

Jenny Weeks- 2024

My Life

I really am ageing!! Sometimes goes on paper.

Legs aching spirits low
Right now no place to go
I've tried to be healthy
Rather be wealthy
With a plane to take me away
To sea sun and sangria I say
So tried digging the garden too
Not good at my age, bad it's true
I've battled with leaves, to go in a sack
They laughed at me and came right back
In the wind, flew over the garden wall
Over they went only to fall
Back where they had started Oh I give up!
So then I carted earth and potting stuff to plant
But back to my problem I can't
Cause my legs are aching
Think I'll do some baking.
(only not good at that either)

Jenny Weeks - 2024

The Sculpture

This Story is pure fantasy.

Jim opened his eyes, he felt totally exhausted, drained, he could not go on, then, as he looked before him it was there the most amazing sculpture he had ever seen, and it was his. it must be, the sheer beauty of it was overwhelming.

How did it happen? How did he create such beauty,

He was in his workshop, his hands covered with the detritus of the completed sculpture, as he looked down he could not remember forming it at all. Nothing!

His mind was a total blank, the last year had been the worst time ever, his wife of five years was suddenly gone. It was quick they said, she did not suffer any pain they said, but what about my pain, she was so young so much to look forward too, she had decorated the small room ready for their growing family.

Also she was a brilliant sculptor, much better than him by far, they had studied together. The sunbeams shone through above him, the sculpture seemed to take on a life of its own, sunbeams danced over it and above and throughout the form, the child seemed to smile from the woman's naked form her arms firmly around it forever.

Through the bend of its arm a beam of light piercing in its intensity, almost trying to connect with him, it shone across the room in a straight line, the sculpture seemed to smile at him, his pain felt lighter, less even, he knew that at that moment she had guided his hands. He followed the rays to the direction of the baby's cot, then a child laughed at the twinkling sunshine trying to catch the sunlight as it passed over its hands.

Looking the image of her mother she smiled at him, Jim smiled and picked up his precious daughter .... his gift.

❤️

Jenny Weeks - 2024

216

I Wish ..... Or Do I?

I wish I was a singing star with admirers left and right
Dressed up in tights and spangles (hehe what a sight)
Me I'm over 75 now and really don't care a jot
Let's face it can't worry about what I've not got!
I droop a bit in places, I'd rather you did not know
But then of course, I do not have them all on show
Some people have long legs right up to their bum
Mine's the other way bum hangs to legs – and tum
But really I should not complain – they still work
I should say now, please try me with a fork
I think I'm done, it's took many a year
Cannot go backwards anyway I fear
So I need a fella to tell me I'm nice
He could add to my world a little spice
So what if I'm wrinkly, not much in the coffers
Anyone out there to put in some offers??

Jenny Weeks - 2024

A New Tariff ...

My day started ok but went downhill
I have to change my tariff,
Now I will lose the will to live, it all took so long
Years ago one phone call now it goes wrong
We have to talk to a computer I get cross
They message back, now I'm at a loss
We'll pass you on and register your complaint
Says the computer – via India – to me, a Saint
But only because no-one listens at all
So being angry, saintly, I head for a fall
Suddenly after 78 mins of being cross
Came a voice, can I help, please SOS
In two minutes flat all was sorted for me
Could have kissed him, took him for tea
Even breakfast .... ok there's limits!!

Jenny Weeks - 2024

The Spider's Visit

The other day a spider entered my house
Big as a tea plate, well it looked it, the louse
I didn't want to harm it, so got out my mop
Put him on top, he did not like it a lot,
So in the garden he did go, wriggly was he
Poor little thing so small, what will be will be,
He's probably waiting so he can get back in
Him and me do not get on, killing would be a sin.
He might be a she with babies in a cluster,
So here I am waiting with my courage to muster.
The next time it comes, I will do the same,
It probably thinks it is all a game.
So game on spider, you must agree
Though you like my home you're not invited to tea
There is a chance if you try again today
I'll squash you dead … no other way!

Jenny Weeks - 2024

Illustrated by Jenny Weeks

The Lottery

Oh, this is me to a 'T'.

I think I've won the lottery in fact I'm very sure
Trying to remember numbers as I go out the door
I am sure it was my husband's birth, maybe mine
Pretty well decided I'd used mine well the sign
Scorpio in the paper said my luck was in this week
All the birthdates in, was asked mine, the cheek!
I struggle with excitement, just in case of course
Rush to the counter hand my ticket say with force
I think I've won the lottery, the lady said "why's that?"
The numbers seem to match in my head, then fell flat
What do you mean not this week, I'm sure it was a win
With what I had planned it really would be a sin.
There were holidays planned and the car nearly bought.
I had spent the money, new house, Disneyland I thought
The children would love it, let's face it, it seems
The luxury of a wealthy future is only in my dreams.

Jenny Weeks - 2024

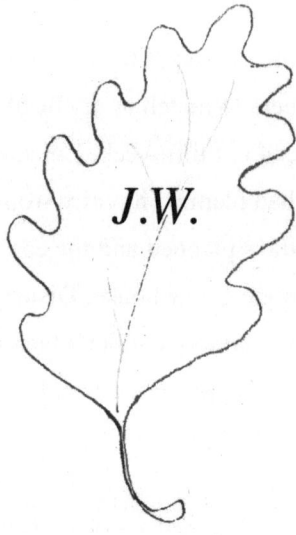

A Group Effort...

And one more poem, to finish off...

Hedgehog

The first two verses of this poem were sent in to the Liden Writers' Group by Margaret Fryer, the wife of one of our members, with an invitation for members to add verses at will.

I think I have a stalker,
So this is what I sing:
If you're born with prickles, girls,
Prickles are the thing! *(Margaret)*

Better than a hat-pin,
Better than a whistle,
If you have your prickles, girls,
You can make 'em bristle! *(Margaret)*

Better than a darning needle
Better than a thistle
With those prickles girls
You can make 'em grizzle. *(Jenny)*

Better than a running stream
Better than a ripple
If you have those prickles girls
You can make them tipple. *(Ann)*

Alright, alright said Spike
No need to be so pointy
Standing there with pins for hair
Acting like the Almighty *(Graham)*

Keep those spikes on, Spike me lad
No need to get so scratchy
No one likes a hot-head hog
Whose fleas are so damn catchy. *(Rosemary)*

Liden Writers' Group

Liden
Writer's
Group

From Little Acorns …

About Swindon 105.5

Launched in 2008, SWINDON 105.5 has remained passionate about supporting and promoting the written, spoken, sung and performed word. This is achieved through training and development, courses, interviews, and enabling studios to be used by creative groups, which continue to develop in size and initiatives.

As a totally inclusive and accessible radio station, thousands of people of all ages and abilities have come through our doors developing confidence, skills, helping with education, towards employment or volunteering, even joining the SWINDON 105.5 team. You can find us on the Web at SWINDON 105.5 | It's your local | Wiltshire, England (swindon1055.co.uk).

As a not-for-profit organisation raising money to provide its service to the community, we appreciate the need for support of essential services like Prospect to gain funds from a wide range of sources. Your support for the writers in turn supports this key service provision and we are very excited about their publication.

Shirley Ludford, DL
Station Manager and
Broadcaster

The Queen's Award
for Voluntary Service

About Prospect

Since 1980, Prospect Hospice has provided dedicated end-of-life care to local people around the clock, every day of the year.

The charity provides a range of services to support around 1,800 people each year to live independently for as long as possible and cares for people in their own homes as well as in the hospice based in Wroughton.

Care goes beyond providing a nice setting for people to spend their last days, and extends to a range of support services including therapy support to assist with breathlessness and fatigue and family support to help with bereavement. All care is tailored to the patient, asking them what matters to them, to ensure care is truly personalised.

All of this is provided free of charge, with no cost to patients or their families, thanks to the generous donations of local people, helping to raise £8.5 million each year to ensure anyone, anywhere can receive outstanding care at the most difficult time.

Tina Bennett, Communications Team, Prospect Hospice

Photo courtesy of Prospect Hospice

Acknowledgements

Our thanks to Shirley Ludford and all at Swindon 105.5 Community Radio for their help and encouragement in producing this book.

Particular thanks are also due to Irene Berridge, the founder of our group.

Also to Ann Perrin, a former member of our group, for providing the audio-recorder that we use for our recordings.

And to each other – for the merry times we have at our meetings!

Contact

To get in touch with the Liden Writers' Group, email us at
lidenwritersgroup@gmail.com

BV - #0279 - 010925 - C0 - 229/152/13 - PB - 9781917573139 - Gloss Lamination